Return To Play

Brandi Heather

To Paige

Love your play Fire

Spirit!

Bandi

Copyright page info

Return To Play:
Rebuilding, Resilience, Risk and Reconnection

Publisher: Brandi Heather
ISBN 978-1-7773527-0-7
Canada
Some names have been changed to protect the identity
of the individuals or organizations.

Editing by: Kristine Johnston
Cover Art by: Predrag Markovic
Book Design and Illustrations by: Predrag Markovic
First Printing 2021

Dedication

My life started in paint and wood and mud pies and folk songs and playhouses. At least that's how I choose to remember it. When I heard that there was such a thing as "A Creative," it was like someone had created a new label for me – like a new hair colour, title, or colour in the rainbow. This one was mine … and there were others: not just creative people but "Creatives."

This is why I show up every day … because that "creative", the play in me has saved my life more than once. It has not just been an incredible sense of what is possible with paint and clay or how to make anything with a pool noodle and a popsicle stick. It's more than that.

I'm here, for you and for me…

This book is dedicated to my mom, the strongest woman I know, two amazing kids, who I hope I am building the road for, and Ken Heather, the love of my life, who helped me find my way and taught me I am enough.

Thank you for those who paved the path before me and who continue to allow me to walk alongside them.

Return To Pla

Rebuilding Resilience,
Risk, and Reconnection

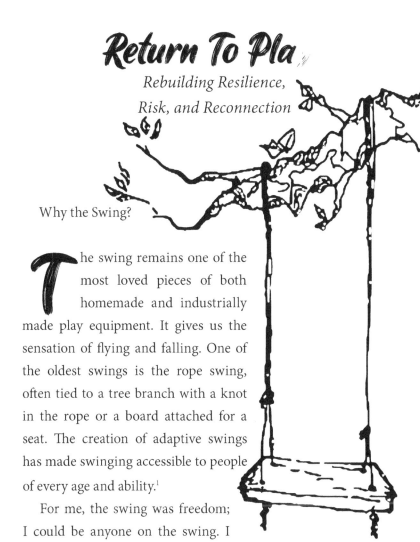

Why the Swing?

The swing remains one of the most loved pieces of both homemade and industrially made play equipment. It gives us the sensation of flying and falling. One of the oldest swings is the rope swing, often tied to a tree branch with a knot in the rope or a board attached for a seat. The creation of adaptive swings has made swinging accessible to people of every age and ability.[1]

For me, the swing was freedom; I could be anyone on the swing. I could lay my head back until I was almost upside down, and I could swing it right to the top and jump off. I loved and still love the sensation of swinging.

The Play and Playground Encyclopedia states that: besides being an enjoyable activity for children, research supports that swinging is very beneficial for children's physical, social, and cognitive development, and can also be used in therapeutic situations. Physically, children develop gross motor skills – including locomotion, balancing, and body coordination – as they run and jump into swings, push others, develop pumping motions, and jump out of the swings. They also develop fine motor skills, including hand, arm, and finger coordination, grip strength, and circling motions of their arms and legs.

Although swinging can be a solitary activity, children usually enjoy swinging together. Since there are usually a limited number of swings available, children learn cooperation, taking turns, and sharing. Swinging can also prompt competition between children to see who can swing higher. Children's social and emotional development is enriched by their social interaction with others. Younger children especially enjoy interacting with an adult or older child when being pushed so that they, too, can swing. Once the child has achieved the skills to swing on their own, scaffolding is no longer necessary.

Swinging can aid cognitive development as children engage in dramatic play using their imaginations to pretend to be pilots or astronauts, for example. This pretend play helps children create a mental picture of an object that is not really there.

Sensory stimulation is especially affected by swinging. For children to successfully acquire the necessary skills to respond to movement and gravity, they must develop their vestibular coordination, proprioception, and visual perception. Swinging helps in the development of these skills. Vestibular coordination involves the inner ear and senses movement of the head to interpret speed and direction of movement. The proprioceptive system receives information from the muscles and joints and aids in balance and body awareness. Visual perception is also developed as children swing and learn to interpret what they see while moving. Children who have difficulty with sensory integration can be helped by therapists who use various swinging activities to stimulate the senses.

The ability to swing independently follows a progression of overlapping swinging skills. Beginners need assistance to sit on the swing and move, and they prefer swinging at lower heights. As children get older, they can lift themselves onto the swing and propel themselves without assistance. Advanced swingers have good balance and have learned the smooth and fluent movements necessary to elevate them to higher heights. The successful coordination of bending the torso and pumping the legs back and forth gives children confidence and encourages them to try risk-taking behaviours, such as jumping from the swing while in motion or standing on the swing.[2]

As an adult, I still go to the corner park and jump on a swing to revive my mind and body. Even though 1,000 things have changed, it takes me right back, and I am a kid again, the real me, in play.

Table of contents

Introduction

When was the last time you did something so good, that gave you so much joy, that you lost track of time? I don't mean that you put your phone down or didn't look at the clock; I mean you didn't care about the time. You were fully engaged and enraptured by the moment.

I'm going to give you a minute here because, for some people, there was a moment that they stopped playing and didn't realize it was the last time.

You see, play is this wonderfully universal thing … you can travel anywhere in the world and see people play – all people. It is one of the universal pieces of our shared humanity. You don't need language to share it or vision to see it. It has its own heartbeat. "In play" is where you are not only enjoying moments but using them to connect to your diverse strengths and talents and the collective strength of others. You will discover that being "in play" means something different to everyone; however, there are a few vital elements. Play is:

- Freely chosen. This is something you choose; no one can tell you that you have to play. If you feel burdened by the ask or the task, you are not "in play."
- Timeless. When you are in play, it has a sense of timelessness. You will often say, "Where did the time go?" or "I haven't looked at my phone for hours!"
- A creator of belonging and connection. Either by yourself or in a crowd of a thousand people, when you are "in play," you feel that you are meant to be there; the play leaves you feeling *this is where I belong.*[3]
- And risky. Play asks you to risk a little of yourself to become more yourself in the process.

" And risky. Play asks you to risk a little of yourself to become more yourself in the process."

Play is as variable as people themselves; holding it down to a single definition and framework negates the purpose. When you see it, when you feel it, you will know it is play.

"Play is how we revel in change, agility and create placidity … play is the root of creative confidence. Play is curiosity, wonder, discovery, invention, empathy, connection, and invitation." – Kevin Carroll[4]

Return To Play rebuilds the way we develop resilience, risk experiencing and embracing something new, and guides us as we learn to reconnect to our collective strength.

Rebuilding

Why Play? Why Now?

> "Cotton candy lava soup," she said, "that is what I am making for my dinosaur and his friends." Armed with three plastic animals, a cotton ball, a plant pot, pipe cleaners, and some clay, a 5-year-old can imagine the solution to any problem. I asked, "How will the dinosaur get across the lava to his friends?" to which she replied without hesitation, "I'll build a bridge, or a boat, or the swordfish will carry them. Lava can't hurt them if they drink water."

Why play? Why now? Because innovative solutions, resilience, and connection live and grow when we can imagine outside the box.

Is it possible that play is the answer to some of our most significant, complex social challenges? Is it our fear of play that is keeping us from revealing our potential? When we protect people from feeling and falling, we protect them from self-care and coping. We limit the potential for ideas that can create change and transformation. When we take risk and play away from people, we also take away all the joy of finding out who we are and how we navigate life when we fall down.

Our likes, dislikes, and greatest strengths lie in how we navigate survival in quickly-changing circumstances. Adversity creates flexibility, and that flexibility fosters creativity, change, and advancement.

" Adversity creates flexibility, and that flexibility fosters creativity, change, and advancement. "

Many people relate play to silliness or a chaos-filled space without limits or control. However, play is respecting that each of us experiences it differently and if we can begin there, we have a starting point.

For example, do you know why it's so hard to capture real play for social media? Typically, we don't stop to take a picture when we are in play because it's the moment that counts. We have lost that by capturing every moment on camera. Play is a whole-body experience; you need your whole self to truly participate.

Consider who you play in front of. Who is it that you let in close enough to know the way you like to play? Do you even consider sharing your playful self in the presence of strangers? And yet, watch people interact with babies, making funny noises, becoming new

" This is the change I seek to make … let's tear off the caution tape and show the world our playful, creative, abundant self!"

characters, and using silly voices … why? Because babies give us permission to play – it's like they come without the caution tape of adulthood and seriousness. This is the change I seek to make … let's tear off the caution tape and show the world our playful, creative, abundant self!

Seth Godin, entrepreneur, public speaker, and author of 19 best-selling books, made time for me in his schedule to talk all things play. During our conversation, he shared that,

It's like many of the most important things in our culture: we don't understand the word; we don't understand what marketing means and we don't understand what play means. So, let me tell you what I think of when I think of play because it might not be the same as you.

When my kids were growing up, a kid down the street was the most intense competitor I had ever seen. He challenged every ref's call and was in every kid's face. If he didn't win, he was upset. I don't think he ever once played a game. Again, it has nothing to do with whether you get money for it or not. Play is a willingness to not win and still be okay with the journey. That's what it is for me.[5]

I asked Daniel Pink, New York Times Bestselling author of *Drive, When,* and *A Whole New Mind,* what he learned in play as a child that he still uses in his work today, and he told me, *Self-direction. When I was growing up, adults weren't nearly involved in kids' lives as they are today. That meant we had plenty of leeway to organize our own games and make our own rules. The skills I learned playing touch football or pickup basketball or dice baseball — from organizing teams to mediating disputes — turned out to be more valuable than I ever expected.*

When I suggested that play could be the answer to some of our most significant, complex social challenges in the 21st century, he agreed in part, and proposed that *the key is that play involves both taking risks and assuming good intent on the part of others. Both of those are in short supply today. But if we rehabilitate play, we might simultaneously resurrect our ability to get along and trust each other.*

" But if we rehabilitate play, we might simultaneously resurrect our ability to get along and trust each other. "

When I asked if it is possible that our fear of playing is keeping us from revealing our full potential, he agreed. *If we don't play, we don't experiment. We don't take risks. We don't try new things. That can be suffocating, just as play can be liberating — a burst of psychological, social, and emotional oxygen.*[6]

Play is where we learn that curiosity is discovery, and discovery can mean transformational change. Play has a lifetime of effects on our physical, cognitive, and social-emotional health and wellness. Our access to uncontrolled or unknown situations in play develops our skills for coping through our lifetime. We see increasing evidence that free play reduction causes significant physical and mental health challenges, both personally and professionally. If we look at exposure to play and risky play, we see that "[i]f [a] child does not receive the adequate stimulation by the environment through risky play, the fear will

" This means that without the experience of trying, succeeding and failing, we will carry a fear of the new and novel with us like bricks in a backpack. "

continue despite no longer being relevant… and may turn into an anxiety disorder: fear responses toward imagined or exaggerated threats and dangers that reduce the individual's ability to function despite the individual having developed the abilities to handle these situations."[7] This means that without the experience of trying, succeeding and failing, we will carry a fear of the new and novel with us like bricks in a backpack.

Tipping point

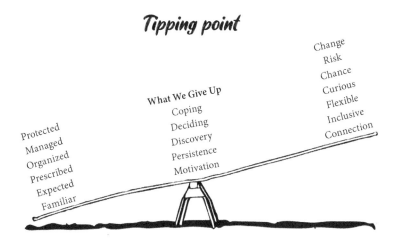

Can you imagine what happens when children are not faced with making their own decisions, falling and getting back up, or playing without adult intervention? We send them off to college or a full-time job and then wonder why they struggle or feel overwhelmed by something new and foreign to them. We fear uncertainty and possibility created by what we don't know. We no longer feel challenged but are afraid of trying something new.

I believe we can build and rebuild our strengths in play at any age, but we need to start by removing the stigma of play as unproductive or frivolous. Play is a place where we conquer our fears and open ourselves up to our full potential. Play can change our social interactions, our physical and mental health, our innovative and creative potential, our drive to take risks, fall, and get up again. Play answers the question: what do we do when no one has the answer?

" Play answers the question: what do we do when no one has the answer?"

The creative confidence to develop solutions to insurmountable issues comes from authentic confidence, motivation, trust, and innovation. Watch children turn trees into tree houses, and puddles into oceans, jump from rock to rock, miss a step, and get back up. Now consider what you experience when someone loves the work they do. What do you feel like in their space? What do you see, hear, and say after encountering people who love and are good at what they do? They are "in play" physically, cognitively and emotionally; they are invested. What if we could build or rebuild the place where we are most open to learning, least self-conscious, and our most authentic self?

We are only brushing the surface of some of our most difficult societal challenges because we try to overcome them without exploring our full potential. Play gives us perspective and experience. However, play is hard work for many people. We often have to climb over a mountain of guilt, judgement, shame, and long-held beliefs about productivity and the seriousness of work to even imagine it as a driver for change. But what if we changed the way we think about play? What if we said that play is the catalyst to igniting and developing the "soft skills" that drive innovation, productivity, and passion and focused on developing and growing them?

Play can be the catalyst for deep conversations that reveal others' strengths, fears, abilities, and concerns that might otherwise have been avoided. Play allows us to unravel prejudice, bias, expectation, judgement, and self-consciousness. It creates a reduced physiological stress response and an openness to authentic conversation.

" What if we said that play is the catalyst to igniting and developing the "soft skills" that drive innovation, productivity, and passion and focused on developing and growing them? "

But it cannot do that without the foundations of trust, respect, connection, and belonging; that's where rebuilding happens. Play disrupts our standardized way of looking at the world – it invites us to change without shaming. It invites dreaming, make believe and creative possibilities.

"The result [of play] is that we stumble upon new behaviours, thoughts, strategies, movements, or ways of being…. Play is its own reward, its own reason for being ." – Dr. Stuart Brown[8]

People and organizations that can play in both times of challenge *and* success will flourish. This is because they have learned that new solutions – when it comes to doing and engaging – come from trust and a vulnerability to be wrong; from doing things in a way no one else has considered; from building with materials no one else has brought to the table. You see, without a diversity of people, ideas, perspectives, and skills, we stay relatively stagnant; we standardize for consistency instead of breaking out of set traditions and patterns. Instead of embracing change we standardize our efforts and actions and prevent play FULL solutions.

" We can start by building trust because without trust, there is not a sense of safety, and without safety, there is not play, and without play, there is not creativity and innovation. "

So, what can we do to break out of these patterns? We can start by building trust because without trust, there is not a sense of safety, and without safety, there is not play, and without play, there is not creativity and innovation.

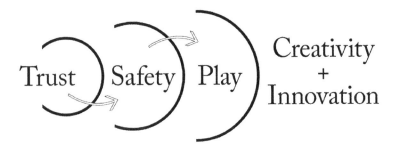

Innovation doesn't just happen. It's the product of creating a safe environment where people feel they can be who they are and do what they love without fear of being judged. Play is part of the recipe for psychological safety. According to an article published in the Harvard Business Review, "psychological safety allows for moderate risk-taking, speaking your mind, creativity, and sticking your neck out without fear of having it cut off — just the types of behavior that lead to market breakthroughs."[9] Fear, then, is creativity's nemesis, the ultimate inhibitor of innovation. When people are fueled with a sense of belonging, acceptance, trust, and respect, the results are imagination, tenacity, and drive.

The Courage to Share and Include

One of my first teaching experiences was in an elementary school classroom. A young man had just arrived from Ethiopia the week before; he was new to the school and the climate. It snowed that morning, and his eyes were so wide. I will never forget the complete stop you in your tracks look of awe and wonder. This young man stood in utter amazement and looked at that white cold magic coming down from the sky.

After the outside break, the students were writing at their desks, and I started to see a puddle forming under the desk of this young man. He had not noticed, and I went over to see if there was something I could do. I whispered, "It's alright," and brought a paper towel, but he had no idea looking everywhere for a source. Just then, he reached into his desk and took out what was left of a tiny snowball. He just looked up at me sadly and said, "this is mine."

He had made a snowball outside and had snuck it into his desk because he was afraid that we would take it away or make him share this treasure. And this snowball was melting right in front of his eyes, and tears started streaming down his face as he felt we had taken it away or made it go away as a punishment for wanting to have it all to himself.

Sharing is a learned skill and practiced skill. How many people remember hiding something you didn't want to share in a place you thought no one would find it. If we have something and believe there is not enough for everyone, we will keep it close.

You will remember teachers and parents saying, "Did you bring enough for everyone?".

The act of sharing and including are grounded in play; they are foundationally rooted in belonging. Do you know what happens to sharing and inclusion when people feel afraid of what will happen next or something unexpected changes their way of living or feel vulnerable to loss or massive change. Sharing and inclusion do not flourish here.

Maybe you remember a time in your childhood when someone told you you had to share a toy or candy or a friend or a parent? Or perhaps you recall being asked to include someone new in a group?

Often, when we are worried or scared, we will pull all of the most important things close to us to keep them for ourselves. This might include snowballs, a best friend, a job, money, cars, food, water, and toilet paper(?). These are often the effect of scarcity or having something in real or perceived short supply. And like it sounds, it often makes us feel scared.

There can be scarcity in physical resources and social and emotional assets, including connection, respect, time, advice and kind words. When we feel that physical or social-emotional resources are scarce inclusive practices like tolerance, flexibility, adaptability, and resilience often go unattended. Taking the time to ask before judging or assuming what someone intends or taking one more minute to explain takes a back seat to keep ourselves from feeling or experiencing scarcity. Scarcity can also lead us into dividing them and us good and bad, sick and well, and the list goes on.

When we feel overwhelmed by our physical and social safety needs, we often move to a drawer system to make sense out of chaos. Like dresser drawers, t-shirts in one drawer and underwear and another and socks in another, we organize for simplicity and structure. Instead of taking the time to consider the perspective of others, their way of knowing, understanding or doing, we put people in drawers, just like when we fold our clothes and put them away. Why do we do that? So we know where things are. It's predictable and sure.

When we are overwhelmed, we go to a drawer system.

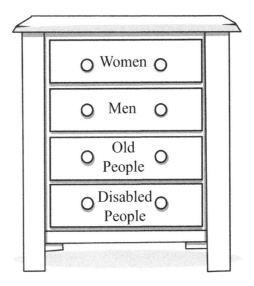

Young people are this..

Old people are that…

Sick people here…

All the people from that place…

All the people I don't know…

All disabled people…

All gay people…

All men…

All women…

All homeless people…

All front desk people…

All administration..

All Men…

All welders…

Do you see what happens? If everything is neat and tidy, we can label it and move on. But life is not in neat drawers, it is messy, and we learn our skills for messiness in play.

I'm in the white, cisgender, female, straight, privileged, mom, artist, author, business owner, teacher, mentally ill, short (but sharp dresser) drawer. But it depends on the lens you choose to see me with and at what moment. My drawer is wonderfully messy, rarely organized and continually changing; it is what makes me resilient and inclusive.

How can we afford to play in a time of scarcity and divide and drawers while hiding our most precious things and protecting ourselves physically, socially and emotionally? I would argue this is why we need to find our play and hold on to it. Play is where we can be authentic, make connections, laugh, and be vulnerable in the face of something new and different. We try and fall and get back up, and if we are lucky, when we fall, someone is there to lend a hand, not caught in drawers and dividers.

It is okay to invoke the "do-over," some of your greatest skills may have been left on the playground; let's go find them.

Moved to Play

He moved four tires, a wood pallet, and four containers filled to the brim with play material across half a soccer field to build the ultimate ship. On the same day, he told the teacher, "My backpack is too heavy to bring home each night." There is a lost (and found) art in bridging movement with motivation and strength with perseverance and determination. Play is one of the most powerful sources of internal drive; no coaxing is required.

As children's time and space to move and play without supervision and in nature decreases, we see a simultaneous rise in the number of children presenting with sensory systems starving for input. Children today are prone to falling out of their seats at school because they lack the physical strength, balance, and endurance to keep themselves upright. According to Angela Hanscom, author of *Balanced and Barefoot: How Unrestricted Outdoor Play Makes for Strong, Confident, and Capable Children,*

> That wide array of movement helps develop a well-functioning vestibular system, along with countless other important physical and mental skills. Now that unstructured outdoor play has become an afterthought in the lives of children, that natural development has gone missing.[10]

Because most kids don't hang upside down, climb trees, jump from heights, or swing until the whole structure sways anymore, their sensory systems are not exposed to or accustomed to change. As a result, children today struggle more with physical and emotional self-regulation as they seek to fill their sensory cup with input. To reiterate, the movement children experience during unstructured play helps them develop a well-functioning balance system, along with countless other important physical and mental skills.

Many playgrounds, daycares, and early learning spaces are "safe" from play involving spinning, chasing, rough-and-tumble, and rolling down hills. Educators are forced to remove these elements for fear of increasing liability issues due to parents who seek "risk free spaces" and want to ensure their children will not play in "those ways." As a result, children have learned that risky play activities are not safe, and in many spaces, they are punished for trying to get what they need. But we need children to move so that they can learn to love to move and become adults who move, too. Where do we find our first movement? In play and exploration. The more we seek to protect children from risk, the greater the loss of independence and drive to discover their own self-regulating processes and body awareness.

The effect of reduced opportunity for play can also be seen in sensory sensitivities in children. It is both ironic and heart-breaking; as we reduce risky play to protect children from danger, we reduce their capacity to develop resilience, self-regulation, and sensory exploration in the process. They are protected from experiencing a difference in everything from ground surfaces to new friends. Children are designed to teach themselves emotional resilience by playing in risky, emotion-inducing ways. In fact, a multistakeholder-developed Position Statement on active outdoor play states that when children can engage in unstructured play outside, "they move more, sit less and play longer — behaviours associated with improved cholesterol levels, blood pressure, body composition, bone density, cardiorespiratory and musculoskeletal fitness and aspects of mental, social and environmental health."[11]

Many people connect this to childhood and children, but what do you think happens when these children grow up? Our bodies are still struggling to navigate a starving sensory system. We seek self-regulating activities like rolling chairs, yoga balls, and fidget spinners. Or, sadly, we learn to seek the opposite: no input, no noise, no movement, and no change. We struggle to pay attention, to stay focused, and we resist activity that challenges us because we fear defeat.

According to the World Health Organization (WHO), "[i]nsufficient physical activity is one of the leading risk factors for death worldwide [and] is a key risk factor for noncommunicable diseases … such as cardiovascular diseases, cancer and diabetes."[12]

Want to know why "Mud Hero," coloured chalk, and bubble runs are so popular? Because they play with fitness by combining physical movement with fun and play. People of all ages can compete at their own level and experience a sense of freedom from the seriousness of "exercise," which opens doors for people to "just try." These activities also have a contagious feel to them: you can get dirty, act silly, get dressed up, and be part of something; there is belonging in these activities. I asked a child what the best part of being in a Foam Fest (a race where people run through coloured bubbles and foam to get to the finish line) was, and she said, "I never knew my mom could play still!"

As the rates of obesity continue to rise, we need to help people find their motivation to move. Not every person fits into a structured fitness regimen or an organized program. But find someone's play – what they love to do that feels timeless – and you have a mover for life!

"'What we really need to do is bring back play for children,' says Dr. Juana Willumsen, WHO focal point for childhood obesity and physical activity."[13] Less than 20% of children worldwide meet the recommended physical activity guidelines, partially because of changes in our movement circles. Movement circles are the spaces within which we are allowed to roam without interference. As a child, my movement circle started at the end of the driveway. As I got older, it extended to the end of the block and back, then the playground, and then the local corner store. We grow these circles over time. Unfortunately for many, our movement circles have not only decreased but diminished completely. There is always someone there to catch you, protect you, and guide you. This has detrimental effects on how children build confidence, independence, and curiosity about their worlds.

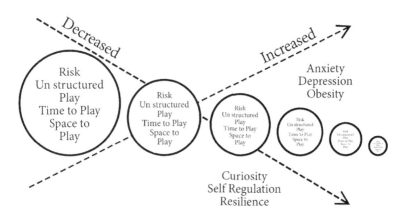

Developmental Psychologist Peter Gray in *Free To Learn* suggests that over the same period that we have seen such a dramatic decline in children's freedom to play, and especially in their freedom to embrace risk, we have seen an equally dramatic rise in childhood mental health disorders.

Five to eight times as many young people today suffer from clinically significant levels of anxiety and depression, by today's standards, than was true in the 1950s. Just as the decline in children's freedom to embrace risk has been continuous and gradual, so has the rise in children's psychopathology.[14]

When everything new is a threat, we are in a constant state of anxiousness; we are surrounded by what scares us the most. Play allows us to experience texture, pressure, coordination, balance, and counterbalance. Remember when someone let go of the back of your bike without training wheels? Our ability to stay upright is created by falling to one side or the other at some point. We are holding on to the back of the bike too long now; it's time to let go.

" *When everything new is a threat, we are in a constant state of anxiousness; we are surrounded by what scares us the most.*"

Physical activity and play are not just for children. Imagine if you loved physical activity and movement like you loved playing as a child? Rebuilding your play starts with knowing and rediscovering those things that give you joy. For instance, constructing, solving puzzles, collecting, and storytelling can all involve movement. Let's combine our play personalities and preferences with our physical activity profile so that, as adults, we don't miss out on the freedom of play just because it's labelled "childish." Learn to dance salsa, skip rocks, or take gymnastics; whether you are 9 or 99, find your play! This is how we will move more and sit less.

When Everything Is Kept Safe

"Can you untie this rope?" A 10-year-old student approaches me at a play event struggling to untie a rope he wants to play with. When I suggest that he CAN untie it, that he is competent, he breaks down in tears exclaiming, "But I've tried a million times!" I have been watching this young man play. I know that he has only had the rope in his hands for less than a minute, indicating that his perseverance and tolerance for trying without help is minimal. Not appreciating my feedback or belief in his skills, he approaches another adult who helps him without hesitation. We often step in to help when we need to support the <u>try</u>.

When we keep people "safe" from experience or failure, we come to believe that they cannot be capable, which becomes a self-fulfilling prophecy. The increased pace of our everyday lives has made us less patient and less likely to invest time and effort in developing new skills. I remember tying my daughter's shoes each day before school, just to get out the door faster. Until one day, when her preschool teacher told me that she was capable of tying her own shoes! I hadn't stopped to consider that was even possible, and she hadn't offered to do it, knowing that when I tied her laces, it meant she didn't have to. I asked her, "Why didn't you tell me you knew how to tie your shoes?" Her simple answer: "You never asked." We keep things fast and safe because the pressure of keeping up decreases our tolerance for change.

" We keep things fast and safe because the pressure of keeping up decreases our tolerance for change. "

In children who do not play, the damage shows up chiefly as a lack of resilience and a shortfall in curiosity. These children also have difficulty regulating appropriate emotions. Nonplayers operate with a limited repertoire of responses, and they tend to substitute shock, fear, or aggression for surprise.[15]

At some point in our lives, for example, we discover that playing with fire can be a very dangerous and painful experience. But we also learn that fire can comfort us and help us engage with nature in complex ways. Until you have experience with fire and choose that you like to be around it, build it, and nurture it, you would never know anything about it other than that it's "unsafe." The same can be said for people; without context, it is difficult to engage, connect, ask, try, falter, fail, flop, and try again. Ever had an awkward conversation with someone new? What if we never had first conversations?

Connection takes practice and experience. Have you ever tried to light wet paper? You know it takes patience and often more than one match. It's the same with people; we are often deterred by the thought of inviting new people into our spaces because we have not practiced getting comfortable with the uncomfortable. When faced with unfamiliar or new, we have to fight the urge to run. Not every spark is a wildfire, but we must have that first encounter, explore how we feel about it, and move forward to know whether or not we are playing with fire.

In David Elkind's *The Power of Play* he demonstrates that

Decades of research has shown that play is crucial to physical, intellectual, and social-emotional development at all ages. This is especially true of the purest form of play: the unstructured, self-motivated, imaginative, independent kind, where children initiate their own games and even invent their own rules.[16]

Yet, we have become afraid of testing new rules and new ways of knowing. Following the rules and systemic patterns of thinking and deciding have become normalized and celebrated, but we long for more. Consider the popularity of reality television shows that seemingly play outloud and outlandishly "break the rules" of social norms like Survivor, Big Brother, Spy Games and Cake Boss amoung so many others. We keep ourselves "safe" from colouring outside the lines by inviting characters into our homes each week who are living in play. Reality television allows us to risk a little through others' experiences, but watching endless hours of Netflix does not count as play.

> *" Reality television allows us to risk a little through others' experiences, but watching endless hours of Netflix does not count as play. "*

According to the American Academy of Pediatrics, "Play is an activity that is intrinsically motivated, entails active engagement, and results in joyful discovery. Play is voluntary and often has no extrinsic goals; it is fun and often spontaneous."[17] When we watch endless hours of Netflix, our brains are NOT actively engaged and, although it can be satisfying to disconnect for that time, it does not have the same qualities of play.

Before leaving Post-Secondary education, I saw an increasing number of students struggling with challenges and choices. They needed to rebuild their confidence in their abilities as they had spent so much time "in safety" before coming to college. We had to consistently reinforce self-reliance, combined with the skills to work in teams or groups. This was becoming more of the job than teaching content. As we made their world safer, I would suggest that we created insecurity about approaching anything that challenged their cognitive, social, or emotional abilities. We had reduced their exposure to risk and difference from a young age, including access to novel experiences that were not adult-led and initiated. The result? Many struggled with adaptability, ambiguity, or having to change directions. When we placed them in the workplace, they found themselves without the skills and tools to persevere when things didn't work out.

We learn adaptive functions for fear and functioning in play. Play is where we learn our physical and emotional hardiness. I put play to the test by asking students to lean into situations that made them anxious in play-based scenarios. In so doing, they became comfortable being themselves, even in front of their peers. I challenged them to talk to new people and see the world from a different perspective. I asked students who clearly stated they were "not creative" to play with paint and playdoh again. Guess what? That resilience – the strength to step in to play even when it feels like a risk – was inside every one of them; they just hadn't practiced it for a long time.

" That resilience – the strength to step in to play even when it feels like a risk – was inside every one of them; they just hadn't practiced it for a long time. "

We have new health and safety challenges ahead of us. So, we are going to need to build both our skills and adaptability to change during challenge. For example, as we face worldwide pandemics, a growing need and desire for the inclusion of every person, and barriers to protecting our environment – just to name a few – we need to practice a nimbleness of thinking. At every age and every ability, we can grow our capacity for new and unexpected things by revealing our strengths in play.

Lonely With 100s of People

When I was 24, I had the opportunity to work in palliative care on a project related to my master's degree; both loneliness and play touched me deeply here. On the first day, I came in ready to put all my "skills" to work, but the nurses put me on bread duty … My inexperience and youth shone brightly as I asked if I could do something in greater connection to my skills. To my surprise, the nurses informed me it was one of the most critical roles on the floor. They told me how making bread in the bread maker and putting the fan on made the hallways smell of freshly baked bread, which allowed many residents to disconnect from the hospital's scent and from dying. The hallways were usually quiet as people did not often have family that came to visit. My "job" was to decrease the emptiness and fill it with connection through the sense of smell.

One of my greatest life lessons happened when she came to the floor. I was at the desk when a woman in her 50s wheeled up to my side to check-in. She introduced herself by saying, "I'm Rose, and I am not coming here to die". I politely agreed with her optimism and led her to her room where she dropped her bags and said, "Time to go shopping. I love a good gift shop!" So, we wheeled down to the hospital gift shop and, en route, she informed me that she had stage four stomach cancer but felt highly optimistic that she would beat it. Her daughter's wedding was in two weeks, and she was attending no matter what!

We toured the gift shop, played with all of the stuffed animals, and made the puppets come alive, but she still did not find what she was looking for. She wanted frames, and she wanted to paint them. We spent the whole day together. She couldn't eat the bread I had made but still insisted that I bring her some to smell, full of butter. Her humour and confidence completely enraptured me. At the end of the day, I offered to go to our local craft store to buy frames and bring them the next time I was at the hospital. She gave strict orders for colours and paint and a gift bag with handles so she could carry it herself.

I returned after the weekend, bags full of supplies in case I didn't have it just right, looking forward to a day of paint and play. A nurse stopped me at the desk to tell me that Rose had fallen into a coma over the weekend. I began to cry and put the supplies away, but she stopped me in my tracks.

"What are you doing? Weren't you going to paint the frames with Rose today?" she asked.

"I was," I replied, "but now we can't."

She took my hand and the supplies and walked me into Rose's room, pulled up a chair, and said, "She can hear everything you say and do, so don't mess it up," and left the room with a smile.

I spent most of the morning painting and talking Rose through each step. The nurses that day taught me that our work doesn't change just because the response changes, that the loneliness in silence is deafening. With wet picture frames on her window sill, and the gift bag ready to create, a nurse came into the room to check on Rose. She asked if I would like to help turn her and, as we did, we spoke to Rose and asked permission. The nurse warned me that sometimes people pass away when we move them, and that's just what Rose did. Play overcomes all boundaries. Surround yourself with people who see the fear and provide a hand to hold.

Play is a universal language that has the power to break through one of the most difficult and prevalent societal challenges we face: loneliness. In 2018, Cigna, a global health service company, studied 20,000 Americans from across the United States. Results revealed that Generation Z is the loneliest among us. Nearly half of

> *" Play is a universal language that has the power to break through one of the most difficult and prevalent societal challenges we face: loneliness."*

all participants reported sometimes or always feeling alone (46%) or left out (47%). That same year, the UK unveiled a cross-government strategy to grapple with loneliness, what Teresa May called "one of the greatest public health challenges of our time." A survey of general practitioners revealed that around 200,000 older people in Britain had not had a conversation friends or family members in over one month.[18]

So how do we move from lonely to play? Finding and returning to play is a common thread amongst people of every age. Consider the opportunity that play has to create connection and conversation. We see it every day; we just don't always capture it. Play does not need structure or planning and can be as simple as a smile to a stranger in line for groceries. One way that I play – though often reserved for small children – is through playing peek-a-boo while waiting in the checkout line. (Hopefully, that's not just me!) How wonderful would it be if we made eye contact and smiled, said hello more often? If, in a single playful moment, we communicated to another person, "I see you." But we don't. We often put our heads down in those spaces, creating an isolated safety zone of disconnect.

Why is it that the 4-year-old waves to everyone and the 40-year-old turns away? We are often so busy in our minds that we shut away input from others, labelling it a distraction to our pace. Loneliness can be created in a crowd of 100s of people and 1000s of likes.

Here is how we can alleviate loneliness through play ... Consider first "your play": something you like to do that brings you joy and a sense of timelessness. This is something you do because you CHOOSE it, not because someone else thinks you should do it or wants you to do it. Does your play involve touch? Physical connection? Touch is one of our greatest allies against loneliness. Many people play to experience touch, which can include holding someone's hand, playing football, or showing affection to pets. If your play includes pets, you know how much being with them can reduce stress and loneliness. A single touch can help us feel safe and connected.

Right now, we are going through a time in our history where many people are starving for touch. The COVID-19 crisis has inhibited our ability to physically connect with others; it has put us at a distance from some of our greatest moments in play. Handshakes, hugs, and physical closeness with family and friends have been reduced and lost, meaning physical play and closeness have never been more important. When we can do so safely, we need to return to connecting through touch.

Does your play include sound or music? Authors of "Music May Reduce Loneliness and Act as Social Surrogate for a Friend" suggest that music is capable of relieving feelings of loneliness and separation.[19] How many people do you know who can turn up the music in the car or on the radio and change how they feel just by singing along? Invite music into your play.

Loneliness can cause physical, cognitive, social, and emotional effects on our health and well-being. Finding time in your day to play, create, build, tell a story, journal, play a sport, or learn something new can help relieve some of the weight of feeling lonely.

Technology, a modern tool to overcome boundaries, has provided us with incredible innovation and advancement. But as our reliance on technology increases, our connection to the value of personal play – play grown from **our** minds and experiences – decreases. Play is often prescribed by algorithm, by the social expectations of the people we surround ourselves with. Loneliness often comes from not meeting the set expectations of the perfect social media post. Through the eyes of a filter, we see people's worlds, project what we think people want to see, and find "belonging" when people approve of what we put into the online world. To cut through this façade, I started to ask myself: *When was the last time I took a picture for myself without the intention of sending it out to the world?*

We often don't see real play in social media because when we are in play, we are too busy to try and capture it … and that's a good thing. Can we agree that as we continue to turn to a screen for connection, we lose a very personal part of us in the transaction?

" *We often don't see real play in social media because when we are in play, we are too busy to try and capture it … and that's a good thing.*"

Technology will not help you paint the frames or hold your hand.

From Playful to Mindful:
Professional Applied Play Experiences

This room is filled with people who work "together" in the same building but individually run their area. As they enter the room, they make intentional moves to sit in a place that makes them feel the safest: they fill the back first. In front of them at their table is a plate with a ball of clay. They have come here with many preconceived ideas about what "Diversity and Inclusion" training looks like, sounds like, and feels like. As we start the day, an uneasiness fills the room, and you can feel the distraction. I ask, "How many of you are artists?" and a silence falls over the room. Not one person in the group declares themself an artist.

We stop and talk about the "title" and what it means. Everyone is clear that "artist" means talent, skill, and experience. We talk (and laugh) about what they think the clay is for and explore their greatest fear about creating something that people will judge. As we talk, we discover that many would have preferred a different medium – a box of crayons or paint – whereas others would have feared drawing something! People share childhood memories or botched play moments with their children and, in 10 minutes, they know more about the people they work with.

We have addressed the fear of being seen as different, their worry about others' judgment, and how that fear changed their behaviour and actions this morning. We discuss expectations and how many could not concentrate on what I was saying because they needed to know what the clay was for. We connect that back to their diverse needs and genuine but silent worry that they are not enough.

We work with the clay, creating simple but tangible objects and, eventually, build an entire story with it. Together, they recognize the power of assumptions, beliefs, and titles and how that can either separate us or create connections through recognizing our differences as our strength. Play provides us with a unique opportunity to find common ground and grow from it. Play is a catalyst for conversations that might never have happened. It is a way to discover knowledge about others that might never have been revealed, including their strengths, fears, abilities, and concerns. Play is the unravelling of prejudice, bias, expectation, judgement, and self-consciousness. It creates a reduced physiological stress response and an openness to authentic conversation, allowing us to move from playful to mindful.

" Play is the unravelling of prejudice, bias, expectation, judgement, and self-consciousness."

After a single day of Applied Play Experiences, we see:

- Increased cues of belonging and connection;

- Reduced apprehension to share ideas and concerns;

- Personal and professional connection to

  unconscious bias;

- Physical, cognitive, and social/emotional openness;

- Increased inclusive behaviour; and

- Increased curiosity about the backgrounds and lives of co-workers.

When we are in play, we are more likely to sending belonging cues to others. This suggests that play is not only a universal language but one that connects us on a level we have only begun to explore. Play bridges culture, race, gender, ability, background, and experience. In play, we discover both our strengths and

" Play bridges culture, race, gender, ability, background, and experience."

preferences. When we play together, we can uncover those same abilities in others.

In play, we uncover our humility. The word humility is rooted in the Latin word *humus,* meaning earth, and *humilis,* meaning on the ground.[20] Play grounds us and reminds us "that humility entails a deeply held belief in the equal dignity and shared limits of all persons."[21] It challenges us to face our limitations and celebrate our talents without the need to feel superior or inferior to one another. When we learn humility, we are more capable of bringing our authentic self into daily practice. Watch small children navigate humility: it's how they discover developmental milestones. Children are not weighed down by the number of attempts it takes to crawl, or walk, or speak; they stumble all the time and always try again. We often lose this as we become more aware of comparison and judgement. Play can build bridges to our humility by revealing what we are genuinely capable of but often hide from others.

Solutions formed in play allow us to navigate many levels of empathy. We start with play's foundation, "my play," connecting to each player's unique, personalized play preferences and personalities. We rebuild personal connection to times we have felt capable, inspired, and without the weight of worry. Together, and in play, we explore play styles and personalities, childhood memories and moments that remind us play is possible. We remember that many of our strengths and preferences were built in back yards, junkyards, and forests.

From there, we connect to "our play." It is here that we can say, "I see, hear, and feel how your play is important to you and why." As we engage in play, we can see many types of play emerge: some people stand in the background, some are the first to join in, some are completely absorbed by the moment, and others are reckless with the feelings and experience of others. We build empathy through shared experience, which helps us invite new perspectives about ourselves and others. We break down stereotypes and assumptions during play as we learn more about our shared experiences, unexpected skills, and backgrounds.

The next step is to create bridges between, "I see the way you play and why it is important to you," and "Because of this, I know you better, trust you more, and am more mindful of your feelings, creating greater connection between us." Like empathy, play is felt in physical, cognitive, and social ways. When we see others in play, it can change the way we feel at that moment. The solutions are always in play.

People need to gain a certain level of empathy and understanding for those they work with to come together and tackle challenging problems in business or their communities. I'm convinced that play can be a key part of creating an effective environment where people can move beyond superficial exchanges and gain empathy and understanding about other groups. This is the foundation for building solutions.

Resilience

How to Introduce Yourself on The Playground

When you were little, how did you introduce yourself at the playground? Can't remember? That's not a memory problem, it's because kids don't often introduce themselves at all. No child walks up to the kid on the slide, stops them in the middle of play, and says: "Before you continue, you should know I am George, and I live at number 67, it's brown with white stripes, my parents are Marnie and Pete, and I will be available for play for approximately 45 minutes today." The playground was where we figured out our space; we navigated unknown kids, often unexpectedly, in new situations.

As we continue to set up and control every play opportunity and experience, the unexpected or uninvited opportunity is reduced. As control and safety are increased, our tolerance for newness and novelty is reduced. How do you experience something novel and unique? The answer depends on the individual. Play creates space for experiencing wonder and imagination but also things and people that are different and new. Imagine what would happen if nothing mysterious or unknown crossed your path until you were 18 years old? Everything new would make you anxious!

In Dr. Stuart Brown's book *Play: How It Shapes the Brain, Opens the Imagination and Invigorates the Soul*, he says,

"People who are play deprived also tend to be inflexible, especially when something surprising happens. Novelty is unpleasant when you are unprepared for it or missing the spontaneity that helps you enjoy or learn from surprises. They tend to be rigid and easily startled and will react with hostility or withdrawal rather than joy."[22]

We cannot lean into the unknown without practice. Remember hide-and-seek? I never loved hide-and-seek because my experience told me that I would find a great place and then wait, hardly breathing while I could hear the seeker walk past. Eventually, they would yell "Gotcha!" and scare me right out of my stillness and stealth. My heart still races when I think of all the little spaces I acrobatically crammed myself into. But it was practice; we practiced getting lost (and found), critically thinking about where to hide and how to stay quiet. We negotiated who was "it" first and when the game ended (sometimes leaving players to hide for much longer than expected).

What if we could take that skill and continue to practice it today? I don't mean giant games of hide-and-seek on multiple floors of an office building. (Although I could!) What I mean is that we need to continue to practice the skills of gameplay, strategy, and preparedness for what is around the corner. Let's practice active curiosity. Let's choose to be curious without judgement. Can you imagine if we could teach people to ask with curious kindness before making assumptions or drawing conclusions about people? Can we stop assuming we already know what the other person is thinking before starting the conversation?

" Let's practice active curiosity. Let's choose to be curious without judgement."

I often tell the story of introducing people to my dad for the first time. My father, an artist and graphic designer, has multiple sclerosis, and when I was in my 20s, he had minimal movement in his hands. I would always tell interested suitors, "My dad will not be able to raise his hand up to shake yours." Inevitably, they would walk up, introduce themselves, and reach out to shake hands. (Nervousness overwhelms our logical brain.) They would reach, and my dad's hands would stay still. He would often respond with humour about his hands not working today, and most people would lean in to touch a shoulder or reach down for his hand. But sometimes, feelings of embarrassment and fear would overcome them, and they would stand without reaction. This is where I learned curious kindness. What you fear is not knowing or doing it wrong, which can keep you from understanding and connecting to the person rather than their disability.

Curious kindness is a practiced skill. Actively seek opportunities to practice curious kindness with people outside your circle of influence. Ask first what they think, and then wait. Actively listen without adding your ideas or solutions. Like you did on the playground, embrace uncertainty and the company of strangers and ask uncommon questions from a different perspective. Ask first to understand who they are before telling them who you are. We are not our titles, what we do, or where we work. How would you introduce yourself if you took those things away? That is your playground introduction.

12 Plastic Frogs: Why People Stop Talking About The Unexpected

When you enter the room, no one is speaking. Twelve plastic jumping frogs have been placed purposefully in the middle of the table within everyone's reach. As we begin the workshop, one person reaches out to one of the frogs and uses it to fidget during the introductions—finally, permission to touch—*then another after another.*

Do you know how many conversations we can start from the question, "Does anyone want to know about the frogs?" With most hands rising, I ask, "How many people wanted to play with them?" Again, several hands go up. So, why didn't attendees just pick them up and play? Because even though it is just plastic jumping frogs, people still worry about what others will think, how they will be perceived, and the consequences of those actions. People tell me that they had to sit on their hands to not play with them. I also hear about the fear of having them jump off the table accidentally and then having to retrieve them from someone else's space. This can occur with people who work together every day and with people who have never met. But there are those who brave reaching out to play with them, which leads to more discussion about environments that support risk and challenge. What creates the courage to play?

Applied Play Experiences are intentional; they build trust, empathy and connection. Still, they are the foundation for challenging discussions on serious topics including, but not limited to, inclusion and exclusion, disability, bias, psychological safety, and culture. Play leads us to an authentic space where we act and react unfiltered, where we reveal our most unique strengths and challenges. From here, we can demonstrate what is possible and explore ways to create spaces characterized by belonging and inclusive culture.

We can also address topics from trust and respect to shame and accountability. Play allows us to explore what we wanted to say but didn't. It's often difficult to tell business professionals that we get to the heart of diversity and inclusion education by tapping into and using play as our toolbox. To bring a diverse group of people together and find a common starting point, you have to start with something they can all relate to. Whether you stand on the outside of the play and look in with concern for purpose and structure, or you dive right in, you tell a story with your actions. But now that we have a starting place … why jump in? Why stand back? We start where the difference is safe, and we move to places no one expected to go.

When we re-learn to play, we practice our skills for:

- Generating new ideas and testing ideas outside the obvious answers;
- Invention and curiosity in the presence of ambiguity;
- Reconstruction and resourcefulness;
- Working in uncertainty and exploring the unknown; and
- Risk and determination to try something new.

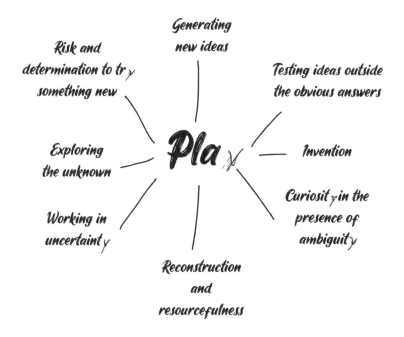

Can you imagine if we had the energy and passion of a child telling you a story about their day? How many people have said, "If only I could bottle that!" We **can** bottle it, but first, we have to find out what makes us *that* excited to share. Show-and-tell is the perfect example. Remember when it was **your day**? The excitement of bringing YOUR THING! What are you so proud of that you would love to bring to work, family reunions, classrooms, or coffee dates? If you can't imagine what that is, you need to practice! Start with objects; they are way easier! What is one thing in your home that you would love to tell people about? Collections, notes, photos, plants, mom's recipe book, art, mailboxes, fridge magnets, food … the list could go on and on.

The point is, so many people have lost their love of show-

and-tell. We worry too much about what the others will bring, comparing and analyzing until it's no longer fun to share or to listen. The ability to explain something in many different ways so that it becomes meaningful to a listener, to create and tell stories, communicate ideas, and show people possibilities, opportunities, and solutions is a show-and-tell skill we still need to practice.

Play allows us the cognitive space to let go. Consider how many great ideas come to you in the shower, out walking, or right before bed. This is because we have learned to allow ourselves space in these moments. Our ability to create comfort in and with chaos is a learned skill. In a world filled with near-impossible challenges, we need the cognitive flexibility to bend without breaking.

"In a world filled with near-impossible challenges, we need the cognitive flexibility to bend without breaking. "

Play as A Life Skill

Mom says, "Go outside and play and don't get wet!"

Spring runoff in Canada means rivers of water running down our streets as the snow melts. One of my favourite things to do was to try and control the stream and figure out how to make it flow all the way down to the end of my block. So, I would take a stick, and I would start to break up the ice so that the water would flow, and then two or three other kids from my block would come down and bring their sticks. They got ice picks and other things they weren't supposed to bring, like dad's hammer, mom's rolling pin, pie plates, and boxes.

Together, we would figure out how to make it so that these rivers flowed in beautiful patterns. Kids would come to stop the river at their house with many different items, including the mittens they were supposed to be wearing. In a matter of hours, we would have a complex system of rivers running through boxes and over snow shovels and rakes and mom's favourite Tupperware. And we would be soaked and frozen to the point where we couldn't feel our hands and feet, but we did not go inside. We argued about the way to do things and negotiated our way through it. No adult stepped in. By the time we were done, 10 kids had figured out how to change the melting ice flow and create the perfect damning system using kitchen utensils, sticks, and the occasional schoolbook.

Let's see ... if the world is running short on humanity and resilience, connection and innovation, maybe we need to go back to a place where we found the answers in the process. In seeing the potential of people and things around us not as they are labelled but by the strength that they bring in the moment, we open up the possibility for creative solutions. Maybe we need to go back to the honesty of those discussions and negotiations. Perhaps we step in too often to save and navigate the challenging moments and give up too soon, ultimately making us believe that we can't.

The statistics on mental health and illness are ever-increasing. We now have generations of children who lack resilience, persistence, and the determination to push through difficult and complex problem-solving. Navigating hardship and struggle is a skill first learned in play. What happens when no one has an answer? Play and creativity are so important in answering this foundational question.

"As children, we always had ambiguity in front of us because we didn't have all the blanks filled in. "

However, being open to multiple possible scenarios or answers leaves us clinging to the sure and stable. As children, we always had ambiguity in front of us because we didn't have all the blanks filled in.

For example, children often fill in the blanks with words that make sense to them, sounds they believe they heard. They will try the word spaghetti and land on "magetty." If we leave it alone, they will eventually find their way to the correct pronunciation. But we correct it because it seems like something that we can control in an often-messy world. Leave it! Let them play with it and come to "spaghetti" without adult wisdom. Let kids create and achieve and be amazed by what they can accomplish on their own.

Can you imagine if we allowed ourselves to make unjudged errors until we found the right path? What if we didn't carry around the weight of a thousand voices telling us the "right way?" We wouldn't hold back great ideas, and we would look outside the obvious. We could try something new without the burden of being "wrong." As we decrease the opportunity for unstructured make-believe play by increasing the number of predetermined play activities, we reduce children's ability to learn a fundamental life skill: self-regulation. When toys and technology can do everything for you and everything comes with specific instructions, children lose the ability to create their own rules and regulations.

Make-believe is where children build self-talk. Watch children work their way through a task; the talk is not for you, it's for them. "[I]f we compare preschoolers' activities and the amount of private speech that occurs across them, we find that this self-regulating language is highest during make-believe play," says Dr. Laura Berk. And "this type of self-regulating language... has been shown in many studies to be predictive of executive functions."[23] Executive functions include impulse control, flexible thinking, memory, planning, task initiation, and organization.

Adults use it too. How many people do you know that talk to themselves as they work? It helps us work through processes and manage our emotions. Think of it as a colouring book versus a blank piece of paper. Colouring books are directive: stay within the lines. They even have colouring pages now where the pens won't work outside the lines so that children can never "fail!" But a blank piece of paper means you have to think of something to draw and where to start; in that, we learn to decide and translate, risk and regulate. Can we deny that we need more people who can create from a blank canvas?

"I'm bored!" has become a common phrase among children of today. As we work to fill every moment of children's lives with content and noise, they struggle to sit still. That seems like a natural progression to me. If I'm consistently consumed, then it's uncomfortable when I'm not. Children are no longer coping with this discomfort by asking new kids to play or finding ways to navigate using their own play drive. We see children's attention spans diminish as they seek constant interaction and entertainment that comes from a source outside themselves.

"If I'm consistently consumed, then it's uncomfortable when I'm not. Children are no longer coping with this discomfort by asking new kids to play or finding ways to navigate using their own play drive."

It's not just children, either. Executives, teachers, and service providers alike dream of workspaces that consistently meet their need for engagement and approval. Productivity is a result of workers who feel both valued and valuable – that is a fact. However, as the amount of time in unstructured play disappears in childhood, less capable people create their own self-satisfaction scale. The sense of feeling disconnected or not good enough permeates the walls of industry and our classrooms because the need for constant input is seldom met. How do we mend this? We need to learn to play

"We need to learn to play with uncomfortable, to challenge the status quo."

with uncomfortable, to challenge the status quo. Find what moves you and play.

Ambiguity tolerance is the ability to accomplish a goal when that goal is entirely undefined and vague. It is a soft skill whose origins begin in play. Research conducted by Harvard University, the Carnegie Foundation, and Stanford Research Center found that 85% of job success comes from having well-developed soft and people skills. The other 15% of job success comes from technical skills and knowledge (hard skills). It seems as though the worst challenge you can give to someone is often one in which the solution is unclear, or the lines are blurred around the process. But ambiguity is an enormous factor in today's world. Consider how we deal with illness that does not have a cause, or the ambiguity in trying to find solutions for insurmountable challenges. Exploration requires taking risks and, yes, those "soft skills."

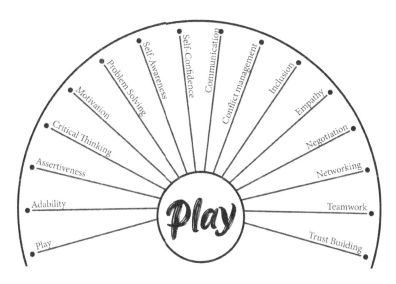

Soft Skills – Which one didn't you learn in play?

Am I Crazy? How a Play Full Mindset Cultivates Positive Mental Health

"Mental health is a state of well-being in which an individual realizes his or her abilities, can cope with the normal stresses of life, can work productively and is able to make a contribution to his or her community. Mental health is fundamental to our collective and individual ability as humans to think, emote, interact with each other, earn a living and enjoy life. On this basis, the promotion, protection, and restoration of mental health can be regarded as a vital concern of individuals, communities and societies throughout the world." – World Health Organization[24]

I was excited today because, although I still had to be accompanied by security, I could go to the art and woodworking space. I have been visited by the recreation therapists who want to know what I am interested in. I can say I have been less than enthusiastic about answering what I am interested in when I feel like I want to stop breathing most days. But after a few days of being unable to leave The Ward, I feel that the possibility to walk down the hallways is a little freeing. I walk into a large room filled with craft paper-covered tables and shelves full of white statues waiting to be painted, and I think OMG, this is not art ... this is paint by numbers!

You see, when you are depressed to this magnitude, nothing feels right and it is hard to see through the fog, which is compounded by changes to medication and neurochemicals that make it difficult to connect your sentences. So, because nothing right now fits the picture in my head, the disappointment is overwhelming, and my sarcastic wit is at its height. At the tables are patients painting, and I think, kill me now ... I am so much better than this. I am not painting pre-set sculptures.

The security attendant asks if I want to stay, and I grudgingly look through the sculptures for something that suits my "artistic stature." I pick a few intricate vases with many details, and think, Not just anyone could do this!! Here is something I can paint to show how capable I am. I'm trying to prove I'm okay by painting the most formidable sculpture. At this point, I don't think I was open to growth or recovery!

I check out a paintbrush, look around for the table furthest away from anyone, and start. Two weeks later, I have completed my intricate vases and must now wait for the art room to fire my masterpiece. Over the past few weeks, I have gained a little more insight into my need to control my circumstances safely; into why I try to surround myself with assurances about my capability and worthiness ... but I am genuinely proud of these vases and am excited to see the end product.

When they come out of the kiln, I am disappointed by their simpleness. I am upset by the lack of evidence of my hard work and dedication to every detail. It looks like just anyone could have done it, and when the woman in the art room asks if I want her to wrap them, I sit down and cry. I cry so hard. I cry in fear and anger and pain and loss and disappointment, and I am inconsolable, so she calls someone to come and get me.

I do not return to the art room for over a week ... And when I do, I look on the shelf at the most unlikely thing I would ever paint: a frog statue. I think, A tacky frog ... perfect! The woman *in the art room welcomes me back. I check out three brushes and go over to the paint and grab random colours. (Something artists rarely do!) And, without hesitation or planning, I splatter this frog with paint – uncoordinated, unplanned, unmatching – blending and painting splatters everywhere! She asks me if I am okay, and I respond, "I'm going to be just fine … I can let go now." It doesn't have to be perfect. I am not perfect. But I am worthy of more than I expected and, somewhere inside, I actually feel that … and I will work on believing it.*

After many tears and laughter, and an hour later, I am done. I ask her to fire it just as it is. The next week, my friend Doug comes to see me. I show him my frog, and he immediately gets it and says, "This is the freedom frog." Yes, the freedom frog indeed. I had rediscovered my play, what fundamentally made me feel alive.

Play can transform our body and mind. When we are in play, our body releases endorphins, which promotes an overall sense of well-being. The reduction in free play for children has had a devastating effect on their physical and mental health. Play is where they learn to navigate emotions, feel competent and confident. It is where we first learn social rules by trying and, yes, failing too. Play has a clear effect on the overall psychological health of children. We see a steady decline in this type of free play in all aspects of children's lives. We are seeing an increasing number of children experiencing childhood anxiety and depression. Peter Gray, Professor of Psychology (emeritus) at Boston College, says:

Children who do not have the opportunity to control their own actions, to make and follow through on their own decisions, to solve their problems, and to learn how to follow the rules in the course of play grow up feeling that they are not in control of their own lives and fate. They grow up feeling that they are dependent on luck and the goodwill and whims of others.[25]

Anxiety and depression often occur when an individual feels a lack of control. Gray believes that the loss of playtime that allows us to exert control over some life circumstances sets the scene for anxiety and depression.

Dr. Whitebread, Developmental Psychologist from the University of Cambridge, similarly contends that extensive evidence has connected the formation of secure emotional attachments early in a child's life to healthy brain development, the regulation of emotions, the ability to show empathy, the ability to form emotional relationships (including friendships with others), emotional resilience, and to playfulness. Children's playfulness, in turn, has been shown to have a central role in the formation and maintenance of friendships, which are of crucial importance for healthy social and emotional development.[26]

"Play is one of the most wonderfully personal and deep connections to who we really are."

Children who are given little practice navigating life on their own – who don't know what they need for comfort and connection – will have less ability to cope and recover when things go wrong.

Where do play and mental health fit for adults? Play is one of the most wonderfully personal and deep connections to who we really are. When we are "sick," it is one of the most challenging things to remember, but finding our play can bring the greatest relief. I have watched it from inside and out. I ask adults all the time, "When was the last time you played?" and "What is your last memory of play?" Many cannot answer me.

What if you went to work or school tomorrow, and your boss or teacher said, "GO play!" What would you do? What do you imagine others would do? Consider your first move. For adults, being told to go play often results in strange looks and hesitation, because we are not used to the freedom to do something undirected, unplanned, or unstructured. Even our physical activity is often carried out routinely, with instructions and parameters for correctness. And even though an exercise class can be your play and where you get playful, it is not recess (free time without structure). An exercise class is not play if you are only doing it because you think you should or are "supposed to." However, when we do something because we genuinely want to, the mental health benefit shines.

When we do something that gives us joy without the weight of judgement, we make space for our genuine self to emerge. That genuine self is the one that gets lost in the weight of mental illness. Psychiatrists and psychologists often miss it in trying to find solutions. Even recreation therapists who get tangled in measuring outcomes can miss the opportunity to find out where the real person is under all the blankets of dark times. At my darkest times, I remember being given a checklist of activities and asked to rank them from 1-10, 1 being the activity I most wanted to do and 10 being the least preferred. Not one of the activities made me want to move from my sadness, yet my team insisted I rank them for their information. I believe mental illness leaves people feeling like they often have to choose from a list of things they don't want to do the most. This is why I believe that returning to play – unstructured, uncheck list play – is vital.

Our logical brain often signals to us what we are supposed to do and what we are expected to do. But who asks us what we are *not* expected to do? What is your list of things no one would expect you to do, but you would love to do? Your mental wellness can be strengthened by living outside what you are expected to do and who you are expected to be. We carry a tremendous amount of expectation, both mentally and physically, with us each day. Some of us have never even considered what it might feel like to drop it off for the day and live without it. Play reminds us that we can separate the expectation from who we really are.

"I believe mental illness leaves people feeling like they often have to choose from a list of things they don't want to do the most."

I was often considered an out of shape, short, and, at times, fat, college professor who taught the "soft subjects" among the fit and fearless expert coaches, exercise physiologists, and anatomy instructors. I was known for showing up to class with carts full of rubber chickens and fish and using modelling clay and plaster to teach connection and kinesiology concepts. I often occupied spaces where I didn't fit, and I reveled in that because it was on my "uncheck list." I taught the value of difference by creating a space that invited and celebrated different ways of doing and being. Being different from what people expect takes energy, but I learned that people felt accepted, comforted, and valued in those spaces I created. Our mental health is as important as our physical health. Find your uncheck list and live a little of it every day.

"Find your uncheck list and live a little of it every day."

Surprise! Unpresented Change:
Time to Face The Mystery Box

We didn't know it would be the last time for a long time. It seemed like in one moment, we were discussing "careful" and "wash your hands," and the next day, it was gone. We didn't realize that we would miss so much; that we would lose the freedom to do what we wanted, to interact freely with others. We had taken for granted touch and hugs and connection and then one day it was gone. These are just some of the effects of the 2020 COVID-19 crisis.

How we deal with massive, unprecedented change reflects our resilience as individuals, as communities, and as a humanity. Very few people like the mystery box – you know, the jack-in-the-box toy with a handle you turn, unsure of when the scary clown will pop out and make a loud noise? But, in our lifetime, we will face moments, events, and people who create in us and our lives unprecedented change. If resilience is built and learned through experiencing change, adaptation, and nimbleness of thought and behaviour, can we rebuild it after we fall down?

"How we deal with massive, unprecedented change reflects our resilience as individuals, as communities, and as a humanity. "

Yes. Increase your personal and professional time in play. It is an answer nobody expects. You might ask, "How can I possibly play in the middle of a war? Global health pandemic? Social injustice? Job loss? Death?" I am not suggesting we break out in a dance party during these times. What I mean is that we need to hold on to play now more than ever and if dance makes you feel strong and capable and allows you to drop your shoulders in these moments, then dance is what you need to make space for. Unfortunately, when crises and uncertainty occur, we often move away from what gives us joy and makes us feel complete. It is hard to find our play in dark places. In fact, we feel bad if we are allowed to play in these moments as it is often seen as greedy or uncaring, but that's why we need to do it. Taking the time and space to play in chaos gives us all permission to let go.

"Even in the worst of horror like a war, children in a moment can enjoy play. Play is a sneaky way of getting to love." – Patch Adams[27]

Have you ever had someone jump out from around the corner and scare you? I bet your reaction was less than polite. Consider how that response causes a chain reaction. When we are scared, we are often the worst version of ourselves; that's human. The way we communicate and respond after our reaction to things that scare us is what's most important. Imagine blindly putting your hand into a box filled by a stranger. How do you approach? What needs to be in place before you put your hand in? What questions do you ask? When do you turn away, and what makes you lean in?

What do you see?

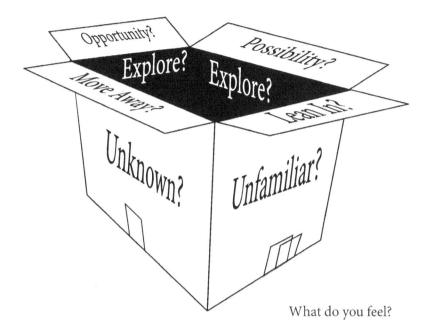

What do you feel?

These mystery boxes are all around us: kids experience them on their first day of school, employees starting a new job or getting assigned a new boss, couples entering marriage, patients receiving a diagnosis, and all of us as we enter a new year or get introduced to a new way of doing or understanding. What do we do to feel those things out before we put our hand in? How do we learn to navigate without experience? We step carefully; we protect ourselves by preparing both our minds and bodies for something new; we reach for steadiness and consistency. When we put our hand in, we will react, both body and mind – even no reaction is a reaction. What we do after we settle, recalculate, and navigate the next move is the essential part.

We cannot change our primitive reaction to the unknownor unexpected, but we can learn to give ourselves the grace to have the reaction and then change how we move forward. This is only accomplished in one way: through practice leaning into the mystery box.

Risk

Play is jumping in the puddle with both feet without the fear of getting wet! Play is training for the unknown and unexpected. Ask a small child to draw a butterfly, and they will try; they will represent what they see in their minds, and do it without thinking about failing … or will they? At what point do children begin worrying that it doesn't look right or may not be the right answer, or even that there is a right answer? That ability to risk drawing a butterfly without a care, without feeling the pressure to do it right, is shrinking. Ask a teenager to draw a butterfly, and they will look up "how to draw a butterfly" on Google. Ask an adult, and you just might get push back or questions and an underlying fear that there's a right answer they don't know. The fear of being wrong and of making mistakes is interfering with our ability to create transformational change.

The "P" Word: The Rise of Perfectionism is Killing Our Play

> *"Every single time I've been in a situation where I had to win, all of me has disappeared, and I can't do my work well, and I don't enjoy being in the game, and it's not a game. And so, I try very hard to always be one inch or one mile back from the life-and-death boundary because if I write a blog post and no one likes it, it's okay because I get to do it again tomorrow. Whereas one of the last times I did a TED talk, they made it into such a dramatic exercise of high-stakes that not only did I not enjoy it, it wasn't as good a thing as it could have been because I didn't get to play. And so, stepping away from the high stakes, we need to be alive and be in the moment; that's what the canoe represents for me. I don't even like canoeing that much, I just like knowing I can play when I am in the boat." – Seth Godin*[28]

When we started AMPED2PLAY, we would discuss where and when we should talk about play. There were certain audiences and individuals that we knew would not connect to our work because the word "play" would stop them in their tracks. We found out, of course, that if you fear play or if it doesn't make you curious to know more, there's an incredible opportunity to create growth! The more uncomfortable it makes you, the greater the impact it can have!

What scares you about the word *play*? What does it bring to mind when you consider stopping for just a moment, doing something that involves disconnecting from the seriousness of what you do? Do you worry that you haven't done it in so long that you might have forgotten how? Are you worried that the things you do to play and disconnect are different from others? What if I told you we can show people's strengths and passions, key components for creating a productive workforce and connected communities, through play? What if I told you that you address complex ideas in playful situations – like diversity, organizational trust, and change management – with your unique talents, creativity, and innovation? Where do you tackle some of your most significant challenges? Where do you think we create our best work?

Play means bringing your whole self to action to face whatever is in front of you. Some of your greatest assets are often hidden under a blanket of expectation and clouded by critical inner (and external) voices. Who do you allow in close enough to see you play? Who would you allow close enough to watch you struggle and persevere? When do you give yourself permission to explore, instead of just completing the task?

We asked ourselves, "How can we create a space where diverse people can feel comfortable developing their play literacy (the motivation, confidence, and competence to play)? How can we create a level playing field?" We understood the concept of Loose Parts Play and studied multiple Adventure and Junk Playgrounds around the world and in history. We wanted inclusion at every level possible, created in play. And so Ramshackle Play was created.

Ramshackle means "poorly constructed or in a state of near collapse."[29] At Ramshackle Play people are in charge, instinctively making hundreds of decisions as they assess and determine the levels of risk they want to take – physically, emotionally, and socially – and mastering, day by day, an increasing repertoire of skills and adding to their bank of experience. Ramshackle Play is a multigenerational experience where people of all ages, regardless of ability, can find space to explore, risk, discover, fail, create, and develop in all areas of their being.

Imagine a 27-foot-long trailer filled with random wood, cushions, tarps and blankets, barrels and boxes, pallets and PVC pipe, spools and string. We call it "play medium." I use the words play medium because it is the material we create with, just like paint, chalk, and pencils are mediums in the visual arts. The play medium in Ramshackle Play is very specific; it's the medium of "something new and different," and makes everything possible at the same time. It is sensory and silly, bigger than you can handle, and small enough to travel; it is lumber and tires, old brass plates, buckets and barrels. It also has a wonderful commonality: in play, it has no set purpose, no name – it is simply waiting to come alive.

Everything that is provided in the play space can be recreated as whatever you can imagine. We leave "perfect" and "expectation" at the door. "But what if I get a sliver?" Then you learn to carry a piece of wood differently, for example, or you experience a sliver and realize it is NOT a reason to stay out of the woodpile. We can't continue to keep sanding off all the edges so no one gets hurt. We need to go backwards and have people explore and discover how to check for risks. Our human resilience depends on our ability to assess risk and hazard and decide how and when to create boundaries and limits. If we sand all the edges, removing anything "risky," we are essentially decreasing our strength and ability to thrive! What we create in Ramshackle Play are transferable skills for a lifetime.

Example:

1.   A child builds a tower of tires,

2.   decides to climb it,

3.   puts their first foot down,

4.   recognizes instability,

5.   attempts to balance,

6.   goes to find something to make the structure stronger,

7.   repeats testing,

8.   eventually climbs up two tires,

9.   realized the solution without adult intervention,

10.   learns they are capable and feels trusted, and

11.   is able to transfer this physical, cognitive, and social/ emotional learning to multiple scenarios.

VERSUS

1.   A child sees tires,

2.   asks an adult for permission and assistance,

3. the adult makes the tower stable or lowers the number of tires for the child, and

4. the child climbs successfully.

5. What does the child learn?

Parallel at work:

1. A person is given a new task,

2. decides on a direction,

3. realizes the direction does not lead to success,

4. considers all other options and tries again.

5. After several attempts, the person is successful,

6. feels capable and accomplished,

7. and discovers new and innovative ideas.

VERSUS

1. A person is given a new task,

2. asks for permission and detailed instructions,

3. does not explore outside the task instructions given,

4. asks many people for the instructions,

5. and is not successful.

6. Someone else must step in to do the person's job.

7. What does the person learn?

•

Overprotection and lack of free play detrimentally change the way our kids face challenge and change. If we take a look at the "Six Categories of Risky Play" identified by Ellen Sandseter,[30] we recognize that overprotection has prevented both children and adults from building important life skills. Let's return to play and explore risk, change, and difference as an opportunity. Our stories are often built in childhood, but consider for yourself the last time you played at great heights, high speed, did something new near risky elements such as fire and water, played in a rough-and-tumble way, or went in a direction without purpose or knowing exactly where you were going?

Consider, for example, how many times you got lost as a child and had to find your way back. Mine was under the clothing racks at Eaton's; I loved the feeling of being under the clothes (which is probably why I still need to touch everything I see). I would hide from my mom, keeping her just close enough to not get "lost," until one time I found myself just that … lost. I still giggle a little when a store announcement booms, "Mrs. Smith, we have your son waiting at Customer Service for you."

From this experience, I learned to keep mom in my sight, the importance of emerging from the clothing racks to get oriented to where I was, and to designate an "if I get lost" meeting place. Unfortunately, as we keep children closer so that they never get lost, they lose their skills for adapting and navigating. It's time to get lost (and found) again.

How about great heights? Children climb trees and other structures to scary heights from which they gain a birds-eye view of the world alongside muscle strength, endurance, and depth perception. What we need to be able to do is give them the confidence to get down. Children often have no problem getting up; it's getting down that challenges them to think critically and problem solve. If we didn't already tell them they couldn't climb the tree, then we jump in to save them from the incredible learning that happens when they need to get down. THIS is one of those life skills: learning the consequences of climbing without a plan for getting down. In other words, how to navigate complex problem-solving. I'm not saying we should leave kids in trees; what I'm saying is that we should help them be the hero in their own adventure.

Here is an example in Ramshackle Play. An adult decides to build a tree fort for some children. Complex rigging and thought go into the building as the children watch patiently for the new fort. Once the fort is complete, the adult leaves and the children start to climb. But they get stuck on certain levels, so the adult returns to lift the children off of the structure. The play lasts approximately 10 minutes.

On the other side of the field, children have found a tree and started to build a structure. They build it to heights they can lift to, step to, climb to. The structure falls many times, but we see determination, persistence, teamwork, navigation, and negotiation. Children build a safe structure and change the complexity of the task after mastering each level. The play lasts for over two hours.

Do you love a roller coaster, or does your stomach turn when you go around a corner too fast? Remember as a kid when you would do something so fast – slide, ski, swing, spin – that you got right to the edge of your comfort zone? That place, where we stop, has been increasingly reduced by the environment we are allowed to explore. But children's drive to explore the edge of their comfort zone hasn't. Their bodies need to explore speed to help them develop depth perception, balance, and stopping. Remember winding up the tire swing and then letting go or swinging to the top of the swing and then jumping off?

We need to do these things, or else we become very sensitive to changes in speed, heights, and even direction. Can you imagine if you had spent your whole life on one level, no up no down, and then I asked you to climb three steps … it would be terrifying! That is what we are doing by limiting the play space and environments for children to explore. They don't want to fall down, and they are afraid to try. If we want children to learn to manage, assess, and work with risk, we need to build adults' confidence to step back and let them do it.

This is not a discussion on helicopter parenting; that serves no purpose for me. I don't aim to set a line in the sand that says, "You are doing it wrong" or "I/we know better." What I want to share is that as we keep kids "safer," they become less safe, less independent, and more anxious. Can we give ourselves permission to push back against the "perfect parent" image and wait 10 seconds before jumping in? Can we choose to expect kids to succeed instead of fearing their failure? It is not easy, as we stand in judgement before a thousand eyes who "know better" on social media but consider where and how you learned some of your greatest gifts. You were probably not tethered by expectations or safety nets.

Expertise   Preferences

Authenticity   Talents

Expectations   Creativity

Unwriten Rules   Reveals   Inovation

Play

Engagement   Connection

   Creates   Trust

Motivation

Physical Cognitive Social and Emotional Welness   Common Ground

Unstructured play tells people we trust them and that they can trust themselves. They can explore ways to self-regulate and soothe, cope and calm, and other life-long skills developed with scraped knees, triumphant towers, getting lost, and imaginary friends. It's time to permit ourselves to play again.[31] The world is a Ramshackle place, let's start practicing our skills to thrive in it. Risk a little of yourself to find yourself in the process.

"The world is a Ramshackle place, let's start practicing our skills to thrive in it. Risk a little of yourself to find yourself in the process."

The Importance of Establishing Foreplay

I want to talk about foreplay. Yes, you can certainly have a little giggle at that one, but I really do want to discuss what has to happen or be in place before we can truly be in a playful space.

Foreplay is defined as an "action or behaviour that precedes an event."[32] Unlike children, we don't jump into play as easily as adults without feeling supported and safe – physically and emotionally. Have you ever watched children as they create a game or fantasy play in a space where there seems to be no set up for play, like hardware stores and junkyards, your office, or restaurants? Just the other day, as I was watching a hockey game in a local arena, I came across a large A-frame sign that said, "No playing. Parents, please keep your children under control in this area." I had to laugh as this space was a beautiful wide-open viewing area with incredible tile checkers on the floors. There were benches to hide under, and the sign itself was the perfect tent for building. So, it was like someone had said, "We set up this great space for your imagination. Please refrain from using it." I giggled and thought, we set up the foreplay … and then said, "No play allowed."

Children don't need foreplay; they can find it anywhere. Adults, however, do need some foreplay. We need to think about what happens before people can be in a space where they can think freely, be themselves, and remove the filters that keep us stifled. So how do you set up "adult" play?

The first thing we know is that play cannot happen in the

presence of fear. Play cannot thrive in a place where our bodies and minds are experiencing fear or anxiety – and I don't mean stress because a certain level of stress can actually drive play for many people. How many people will tell you that their best work is done against a deadline? That they thrive on stress or live for that balance between *oh my goodness I'm going to lose control* and *it's almost perfect?* This is the fear of saying something wrong or doing something incorrectly, of worrying that someone is watching or listening or filtering every answer. This is the fear that causes us to sacrifice what we really feel to please someone else. In these spaces, we will not find our play, our voice, our potential.

The second thing we know for sure is that play is voluntary. It cannot be forced or coerced. Play is a voluntary act, and even though we can set up all sorts of applied play experiences, we cannot MAKE people play. Good foreplay is an invitation. Remember birthday invitations? This was a big deal during my childhood, whether you made them from scratch, with paper and scissors and cut-outs, or you used the store-bought Sesame Street and Bugs Bunny ones. You put your friends' names on them, people you hoped would come, and people you wished would come. And no matter how the birthday invitation routine went, there was almost always someone who didn't get invited. If you've ever been a part of this triangle – the inviter, the invitee, the not invited – then you understand how we can create foreplay through invitation. There was nothing better than finding your invitation on your desk at school or in your schoolbag, and nothing worse than looking through your bag for your invitation, only to find out that you hadn't been invited.

What if we remembered that feeling when navigating complex problem-solving and change management and brought people together into an inclusive space versus a divisive one. What if our invitations, cut out and brightly coloured with sparkles and glue, invited everyone so that the foreplay happens way before the actual meeting or party? You see, the invitation is a huge part of the foreplay for adults.

Have you ever watched on a playground as a parent tries to coerce their son or daughter to ask kids if they can play with them? And then witnessed another child leave play to reach out a hand and include them so that they didn't even have to cross the trail of sand to ask? That brave skill comes from having had another hand reached out to them at some point in time when they were scared to ask if they could play. Create spaces that invite people to use more than their resume talents. Good foreplay creates Braving Connection.

Braving Connection

Braving Connection is the cushion that lines rebuilding risk, resilience, and reconnection. It is not bubble wrap, and it doesn't always protect us from hurt or fear, but if we can practice it, we will transition successfully from fear to function more often.

Braving Connection means asking for help when it feels vulnerable, or you are unsure of the response. It also means recognizing the vulnerability in asking questions and being receptive to the possibility of different ways of seeing solutions. It is practicing both listening and hearing, understanding that a single instruction can have many interpretations.

For example, take out a clean piece of paper and do the following:

    1. Draw a line from one side of the paper to the other.

    2. Draw a circle.

    3. Draw two triangles.

    4. Fill in one triangle.

    5. Draw a square.

    6. Draw a line that connects all the shapes.

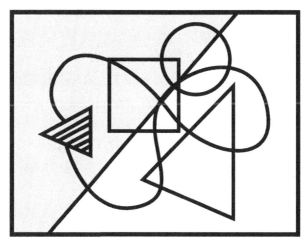

Six simple instructions can create an infinite number of pictures. Braving Connection means recognizing there are that many interpretations, all of which are the correct answer. How many times do we risk asking for help or clarification in fear of feeling inadequate? How often do we feel upset with ourselves for not meeting expectations either created by ourselves or others?

Defining play is like defining joy, love, hope, and so many other personal things. I work with definitions from research with 5-year-olds to evidence and science to the wisdom of people who have lived long enough and deep enough to remind us of life's importance.

So, when we define play, we have to remember that one person's play is another person's anxiety attack. Braving Connection means I am open to understanding and utilizing my play and being available to recognize yours. Braving Connection means being able to follow the instructions (like those above) and acknowledge that you may have:

1. Wondered if there was a right answer.
2. Considered how everyone else would do it.
3. Thought it might be a trick.
4. Considered using different colours.
5. Not completed it because it made you feel childish.
6. Considered what could be interpreted by your answer, suggesting "smart
7. People" do this or "creative people" do that.

If so, you are like so many others I have completed this demonstration with. The exercise is only a demonstration of the creative solutions that people come to using six simple instructions. However, when I started to do it with adults it would create hesitation; they would look at other people's "answer" and even refuse to complete the task. Why? Because, as human beings, we are not only driven to belong, but have become so focused on winning and losing, on coming up with the "correct" answers, that we find it difficult to complete even simple tasks without the fear of being judged as wrong.

When we do this same task with children in kindergarten, we get beautiful creations unhindered by the filters that, as adults, we have learned to put into place to protect ourselves from shame or judgement. What if we could unwind some of those questions so that we could connect, imagine, and create at a greater level? Play reminds us that we can.

Just as this activity was not a test designed to produce a finite number of "correct" answers, life is not a finite game. As Simon Sinek says,

> *In finite games, like football or chess, the players are known, the rules are fixed, and the endpoint is clear. The winners and losers are easily identified. In infinite games, like business or politics or life itself, the players come and go, the rules are changeable, and there is no defined endpoint.*[33]

Braving Connection implies that we open ourselves up to the possibility that there is more to work and play than winners and losers, right and wrong, black and white. Play is the perfect medium with which to start to play infinite games again.

Many play researchers have worked with the definition of play from a thousand different angles and structures. Play is intrinsic and self-directed. It is built and felt from the inside of **people**, and although we can be affected by watching other people play, finding our play is something that we feel with our whole selves.

Play is voluntary; we cannot be forced into it, and we are in charge of ending it.

(Although, I'm sure we all have great examples of how much others get upset when we aren't fully engaged in whatever activity is going on.)

As parents, for example, we are often called into play by our kids; however, while having us be a part of the game of hide-and-seek *is* play for them, it *is not* play for us. For many of us, including myself, we are guilty of spending unconscious time pretending to play, physically in the moment but mentally somewhere else. When we are really in play with our kids, we are present; we are doing something playful for both of us, not just for one of us. When we are not or cannot be "in play," we are often left feeling heavy with guilt because "good parents" play!

We can't always be in play; to expect that of ourselves is not only overwhelming but impractical. But what we can do is be more mindful of these moments and take the time to live in and lean into them when they happen. For me, this is singing in the car. My kids and I can sing in the car and be 100% in the play together. The great thing about kids is that they know when you are in play. They will go back to it a thousand times to feel it alongside you because when you are really in play they feel an authentic connection.

Sometimes just watching play can give us happiness – we don't have to be in play to enjoy it. You cannot be in play if you are not there by choice. Like changing attitudes and behaviours, forced compliance will not change the way people feel or engage with something. However, we can be moved to play by being invited into a space and learning that we can find play within it.

Here's an example from the playground … Have you ever gone to a dinner party and someone says, "Who wants to play charades?" You hate charades. You never know what to do, feel the game makes you look silly, and don't like doing embarrassing things people will talk about and "insta-text" to everyone out of context. Thankfully, someone else has gone first – this is their play, and they love it. They have a thousand ideas, start without fear, and freely laugh amidst the confusion and competition. You sit in the background, watch for a while, and, at some point, you realize that you know the answer and think, How can they not get it? How can they not see? The answer is obviously "umbrella!" And then something happens …

Being around people in play is infectious. It cues a part of our brain that is driven to mimic and imitate. Play sends belonging cues and an invitation to be a part of something even when you are standing on the outside. Belonging cues are key to feeling safe in times of vulnerability; they are "behaviors that create safe connection in groups."[34] However, it is very different to receive an invitation to play versus being forced to play. If your wife pulls you to the front in that same game of charades and says, "You go first!" you will not be in play, for sure. It would be like being forced onstage in front of a crowd of people with a microphone in your hand when you had intended on being in the audience. After that experience, you won't go back to anything that looks like charades again because charades will feel like sweaty palms and fear and embarrassment, which is very different from the feeling of involving yourself when you are ready at a level you are prepared for.

As we build strategies for organizational culture, the parallel is this: we often put people in front of the room with a microphone in their hand versus inviting them to watch from the sidelines until the invitation feels inviting. Not everything has to be an invitation in business, or education, or sport. Still, we have proven time and time again that shaming people into action or behaviours you EXPECT rarely results in optimal performance. Imagine if, in your workplace, you felt invited versus convinced or obligated to look at things differently. Imagine you were invited to build solutions versus being told, "Here is the solution!"

What if we can connect to what makes us feel free, confident, open to new perspectives, and safe to explore ideas. You may think, *that sounds inefficient*, but consider how much time we are wasting right now on initiatives that have to be repeated over and over again because they do not move people; they only change the font.

What if we signalled more often that it is okay to play now, fall down, change directions, do something unheard of, and be different? How long would it take if people felt valued and valuable for them to be comfortable sharing their input? How long would it take to do things in a way that made them feel valued and heard? Building a culture in play recognizes that unless it is YOUR play, we will not throw you on stage with a microphone without strategy and support. Let's peel back the layers and Brave Connection again.

Let's Get Messy - Igniting Innovation and Triumphant Transitions

"I am strong, creative, and powerful because I can imagine outside the lines."

My daughter loves to create slime. If you haven't heard of this, it's the combination of liquid elements – like Elmer's glue, contact lens solution, and liquid soap – that create a sensory circus, which, in my world as a kid, would have been called silly putty. Silly putty was that plastic, stretchy, slimy, stringy stuff that came in a plastic egg and never came out of carpets. If you rolled it into a ball, it bounced, but we were unsure what it was made of.

My 12-year-old daughter and most of her friends make this now from scratch.

They are science experiments gone mad, as they try to create the ultimate colour, smell, and texture to produce the "perfect slime." As they do, my house becomes a combination of plastic containers filled with experiments in "slimology." What I know is that the play is the thing; the mixing and inventing, the finding out what colours are possible, and the creating is the play. When you watch it happen, it ignites every sense, and when it's done, they have created something that they can play with in the way they like it, which is very individual.

But here's what has to happen before it becomes play: they have to crave the sensory experience of this product. I'm not sure how many people I can tell you look at the end product of slime and want to put their hands in, but the drive for this sensory engagement is a huge part of the play. That means play is motivated by a personal affinity for the sensory experience.

We set up a table for slime production in our basement because, if we didn't, it would continue happening in our bathrooms and kitchen! We learned quickly that Megan was very driven to play in this way and that trying to tell her not to do it would have been futile – guiding the creativity and creating space for it gave her the best opportunity to explore. We learned that before she could play, she needed to know that she was free to make a mess in her space and that she wasn't having to hide making the slime. When people feel that they can try, experiment, and risk without fear, they will play and persist until they find that perfect recipe for success.

My daughter has made what she calls the "perfect slime" a thousand times. I can tell you that the end goal was as much part of the play as the process. Children have to be exposed to opportunities to experiment, to try and fail and keep trying.

What does your perfect play environment look like? What needs to be in place so that you can feel free to experiment? What is your "slime", where the process is the goal? I challenge you today and every day to repeat the following:

Fear loves shame.

Fear loves guilt.

Fear loves the feeling that we are disappointing others.

Fear loves anger.

Fear loves escape and avoidance.

Play loves something new.

Play loves something we know and don't know.

Play loves being yourself.

Play loves it loud ... and quiet.

Play loves both silly and still.

•

We need to get messy again, not just in paint and playdough, but with our bodies and our minds! Find something puzzling, create a solution, and build something you never have before but have always wanted to. We see a rise in "Paint nights," which is a great step to something more! Paint nights work because they create an invitation to explore art with the safety net of the step-by-step process for success. But we need more middle ground. We need slime for a lifetime, something we can dig our hands and brains into that reminds us that messy is progress!

"The world is craving invention, creativity, and imagination, but teaches standard and sturdy."

The world is craving invention, creativity, and imagination, but teaches standard and sturdy. Play is a process; you need to create environments that accept a person's play as part of their potential for their best performance.

According to researchers at the University of South Australia,

Creativity and creative development is an essential skill for all our endeavours and relevant to all areas of human activity. It can be regarded as the ability to shift one's perception in terms of how information can be reconfigured to create new models and meanings beyond what is expected, or what are the traditional ways of seeing things, issues, or problems, to come up with new ideas.

They also suggest that

During [creative] play children learn how to work together, adapt to different situations, experiment, explore, problem solve, construct meaning, begin to learn what they like, what they are good at and how to express their individuality and develop a positive self-concept.[35]

What if we afforded ourselves, as adults, the same opportunity? I have seen that when people are in play, we invite great curiosity, connection, empathy, and compassion. We have forgotten that we learn to navigate conflict and manage stress through practice. As adults we seek fast, efficient resolutions and completion. We no longer strive for play, discovery or changing direction in the process. We don't need to bring back merry-go-rounds or long metal slides to practice, but we need to allow people to get lost without always having a map that brings them home. We can't continue to protect ourselves and our children from experiencing life in fear of change or the unknown.

If You Play Your Cards Right (Who is Play Full?)

When I asked Seth Godin about play and the importance of it to his work, he said,

One place we have to begin is either by saying play helps us become more productive, OR the purpose of being productive is to allow us room to play. And they are totally different things.... I bet that in order for you to get gigs, you have to articulate to the boss how this play leads to productivity. Sooner or later, built into that, play is over ... and they will ask, "Where's my productivity?"[36]

Do you trust the people surrounding you enough to play and be playful? Last week, I walked down the corridor of our office encased in a full-body, stretchy blue lycra bag, Patch Adams style, to make sure our team remembered why we are here. I don't expect everyone to do that any more than I think adding a ping pong table to the office answers all of your team's culture challenges. Many people hear "play" and think *lack of productivity, loss of control, wasting time, and inefficiency.* But what we know is that if you allow people to play at work – that means either being or bringing something that invests in their

"You see, when companies bring in the ping pong table without purpose, it's just a large, inconvenient surface to bounce a ball on. But when initiated as a genuine investment in people, a curiosity about who they are, not just what they do, then the play can work."

98

interests by seeking to create belonging – employee productivity, loyalty, and retention all increase. You see, when companies bring in the ping pong table without purpose, it's just a large, inconvenient surface to bounce a ball on. But when initiated as a genuine investment in people, a curiosity about who they are, not just what they do, then the play can work.

How is it possible that play is "working" in all of these spaces and more? Peter Gray's research suggests that,

Adults can test the degree to which their work is play by asking themselves this: "If I could receive the same pay, the same prospects for future pay, the same amount of approval from other people, and the same sense of doing good for the world for *not* doing this job... would I quit?" If the person would eagerly quit, the job is not play. To the degree that the person would quit reluctantly, or not quit, the job is play. It is something that the person enjoys independently of the extrinsic rewards received for doing it.[37]

Educators at Play

> *He made me believe in the value of language. His art was to make you love Shakespeare at a time when you were most in love with yourself. I can still recite* The Rime of The Ancient Mariner, *by Samuel Taylor Coleridge, because he not only looked like he was the "grey-beard loon," but told the story as if he'd been there and wanted us to come too. His play was his work; he pushed us harder than anyone before, but he also taught us to respect and use words with reverence. Thank you Mr. Marshall.*

Treat your educators as though their ideas and energy are a part of them. As vital as the environment and resources we give them is the support to be themselves in play. They will return this respect (for the foundation of who they are) through great teaching and pass forward the confidence to explore, fail, trust, and imagine. only if they receive that support themselves. What we want for our kids is what we need first to give to our educators. Everything flows through them.

"What we want for our kids is what we need first to give to our educators. Everything flows through them. There is a magic to great teaching"

There is a magic to great teaching. It is where we bring ourselves to the table for students and say, "This is me; I am here for you." But we know that many teachers stop teaching in the first two years of practice not because they run out of ideas or don't care anymore, but because they have lost their play. Great teaching is great play. When an educator knows their play, they are more likely to share it. When you give a great lesson and watch a student achieve something they didn't think they could do, no matter what kind of educator you are, you have found a moment worth reconnecting to. This is something we don't do enough.

We often see educators whose play is stuck inside them, overrun by systems, class sizes, and unrealistic expectations of being social workers, health nurses, *and* parents. In these systems, we don't have permission to play; we are often just surviving. Learning can't live here. Seth Godin, shared this memory about play and education with me.

> *The great Lenny Levine who was a kindergarten teacher before he died too young in our local town said to the kids the first day, there is only one rule here which is "you can't say you can't play" you can't say to another kid "you can't play". And he said to the parents every single kid who has ever been in my classes have learned to read "its not my job to teach them how to read it's my job to teach you to be humans will know how to play" I think of Lenny all the time.*[38]

How many great teachers do you know who taught you the value of learning through play? Educators often have this amazing little spark that cannot be put out by the weight of expectation and stress. You will find it in the corner of classrooms where some have been able to bring a little of themselves. They have given themselves permission to play. Watch a new teacher create their classroom for the first time or a seasoned teacher as they do something no one else does because they have earned the right. In our own right, many of us are secret "play hoarders"; we walk the isles of stores and find new ways to mix it up and make it more. But play takes energy! It doesn't come from a place of exhaustion, overwhelm, or being undervalued.

Play is hard to build from beneath a pile of bricks ... what are your bricks?

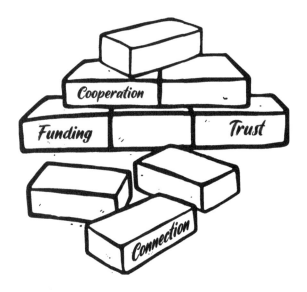

Play in education and learning is not for "off the side of your desk," but so many of us have built it there. I've watched hundreds of teachers gamify math, create concoctions to add a taste to language, build actual towers of achievement for reading or homework, and so much more. What is the return on that investment? One student who comes back to your classroom after graduation? One student who got it? One student who spoke up?

What if we built that play back into our spaces – not because we are trying to meet some unrealistic expectation placed on us by social media to be and do more, but because we wanted to? What if we took a look at what gave us the lift, the spark, the smile that's contagious? The late Sir Ken Robinson, in his book *The Element: How Finding Your Passion Changes Everything* said,

> The fact is that given the challenges we face, education doesn't need to be reformed -- it needs to be transformed. The key to this transformation is not to standardize education, but to personalize it, to build achievement on discovering the individual talents of each child, to put students in an environment where they want to learn and where they can naturally discover their true passions.[39]

I suggest that we include ourselves in this exploration. What exceptional talent, skill, or hobby do you have to bring to your classroom? What are you passionate about? What is your play?

We spend so much time "in process" and navigating systems that we can lose our play, our magic, and the reason we started in the first place. Educators have so much pressure to document and justify what they do and why they do it that the relaxed, playful environment is compromised. We continue to do the best we can for the student's sake while trying to fit into the ever-growing restraints we must work within. The playful mind is a creative mind, which has the flexibility to change direction with confidence and purpose. Imagine how many times in a day a teacher has to make innovative changes in direction, focus, and management? Do you think it's possible to

"The playful mind is a creative mind, which has the flexibility to change direction with confidence and purpose."

do this under the constant weight of *Am I good enough?*

The COVID-19 pandemic has disrupted the education of over 90% of the world's students. It has exacerbated already existing inequalities and magnified the global learning crisis. The future of an entire generation is at risk. But while education is clearly a victim of the pandemic, it is also the solution to the longer-term recovery.[40]

What is your play outside of the classroom that you can bring inside every day? I teach physical literacy: the motivation, confidence, and competence to engage in physical activity,[41] and I believe we need to address the same "literacy" in play. Helping educators discover or rediscover their talents and gifts. Educators of every kind take content and curriculum apart and build the motivation, confidence, and competence to learn. To do that, they need the room to play.

I love connecting with teachers and finding out how they are playing. When you let yourself be wrong, and give yourself the space to learn and teach, then you will also find play in an ever-changing and unpredictable teaching environment. To find the magic in all kids, you will first have to understand what keeps you from seeing the magic in you. Do you worry about making mistakes? Do you fear that you will say something wrong? I have a secret that many people don't share ... it's all right to be afraid, and it's all right not to know all the answers. As educators, let's have honest conversations about every student's diverse needs, about large

"The expectation that we will know all the adaptations, modifications, and strategies is one of the most significant barriers to being creative and finding solutions."

class sizes, and about managing an ever-changing expectation that we know all the answers.

The expectation that we will know all the adaptations, modifications, and strategies is one of the most significant barriers to being creative and finding solutions. Like building a house, let's start with the foundation; let's get some actual conversations started about the challenges and opportunities that an education space can provide. Let's build strong support in understanding, connection, knowledge, and strategy sharing, and let's get away from standardized ways of thinking. No more filters! Every layer pushes you farther away from what's real: real gifts, real strengths, real deserved wrinkles, and natural smiles. Revel in change. Play is agility and plasticity. Take a risk. Ask a question. Ask first what **you** need to thrive, flex, and grow. Consider first **your** strengths and build your house on that foundation.

"Play is agility and plasticity"

Proving Play and Profit for Business

Play and profit? They shuffle in their seats while a curious but cautious manager introduces them to a single idea: play leads to productivity and profit.

Let's go back to the playground for a moment … How many of you built forts? My favourite kind was made out of couch cushions and blankets. My grandparents had the best sectional! It was orange and picky because it was made from wool – not functional for sitting but the BEST FOR FORTS! The key was that this awful material didn't slip, so you could put the cushions just so, and they would always hold. The other great thing was that this couch was in the basement, which meant no adults could watch. This allowed me to create these forts with everything in the basement I could find – my grandfather's shoehorn that looked like a horse, blankets and sheets from the spare room, as well as standing ashtrays and the broom from the laundry room, to prop up things that would collapse. The best feeling came once it was all done, and you could lay on your back inside. It was freedom, mine, hidden, escape.

The next step to great fort building was touring someone else through the fort; showing off what you had built, including all the nuances of the space, sharing your creation with someone who could see or connect with your vision … "Here is my bedroom, the kitchen, this is where the sun comes in, and this is the secret exit in case of intruders."

These forts come in all shapes and sizes and provide a safety net. People still build them all the time; they just don't realize

> *it. It is what good companies create for their workers: a place to feel safe, heard, and included. To build spaces where everyone is allowed to build, create, and fail, to bring all of their different materials (life experiences, beliefs, values, and skills) and use them to build inclusive spaces for themselves and others. People are driven to belong and be a part of something, but building empathic connections comes from seeing that every fort is great – because fort building is personal.*

Many people question how it's possible to even start this conversation with businesses and organizations whose core values are centred on production, shareholders, and profit. Ask someone you know to describe the parts of their work that feel like play. (As a reminder, this is when we feel capable, free to decide, change directions, most open to new ideas, AND authentic.) Most often, you will receive the response that work is not for PLAY.

This is where I believe we need to go backwards to go forwards. We often talk about the ways in which we progress, move forward, and advance without considering that there are skills left uncovered every time we move forward without consideration of where people have been or where they are coming from. But how do we progress from play to inclusion to performance to profit? Through trust.

The Google lead study "Project Aristotle" found that psychological safety – the ability for team members to feel safe and vulnerable in front of each other – was the number one factor that drove the success of its most effective teams.[42]

Research shows a direct link between employee engagement,

performance, and work satisfaction when creativity and innovative risk-taking are encouraged and supported. Yet, "[o]nly 29% of workers strongly agree that they're expected to be creative or think of new ways to do things at work." [43]

When we engage in what we are naturally suited to do, when we use our whole self and our strengths, our work takes on the quality of play. And when we can help organizations see that in play, we have great strength, ideas, and purpose, then we can dig into the reasons why and how your organization deals with:

- Change Management;
- Performance Evaluation;
- Communication;
- Productivity;
- Engagement;
- Mental and Physical Health;
- Inclusion;
- Loyalty; and
- Retention.

Once we can recognize and reconstruct those foundational pieces, then we can construct a business that grows and thrives sustainably. Play disrupts our standardized way of looking at the world – it invites us to change without shaming.

"Play disrupts our standardized way of looking at the world – it invites us to change without shaming."

•

Play emphasizes the social aspect of relationships with employees, building employee loyalty and flexibility. Play recognizes that we are more than just employees; that we have unused skills and talents that could be harnessed to improve multiple parts of our organizations. Consider the employee who is also an artist or a gamer in their free time, or a worker who loves to construct models – take those playful skills and allow people to combine them with their work. This not only increases happiness but also sends belonging cues to people that tell them how valuable their **whole** self is to your organization and its culture.

A business that can play in both times of challenge and success will succeed because they have learned that new solutions come from trust and a vulnerability to be wrong; to do things in a way no one else has considered; to build with materials no one else has brought to the table before. This business invests in and prioritizes creativity, problem solving, risk and partnerships.

You see, without a diversity of people, perspectives, and skills, we stay relatively stagnant; we manage change instead of breaking out of set traditions and patterns. To break out ... start by building trust because without trust, there is not safety, and without safety there is not play, and without play, there is not creativity and innovation.

"You see, without a diversity of people, perspectives, and skills, we stay relatively stagnant; we manage change instead of breaking out of set traditions and patterns."

If we don't have trust, we will build all kinds of forts to protect ourselves and keep others out, and hide versus excitedly inviting others in to play. We need to find out about the people we work with and for so that we know their fort building stories because that's where we will find some of their greatest strengths and skills. But this does not come naturally; there is a process for learning how to use play as a path to performance. We move people from asking, "Why would you build a fort like **that**!?" to, "Why **would** you build a fort like that?" In play, we can move from shame and blame to curiosity and discovery.

So, let's look at an example in business … "Company X" has 50 employees, which must all complete a mandatory diversity and inclusion training module and in-person training. Employees are paid for the time and return to work the following day. Nothing changes. Two weeks later,… still no measurable change in engagement or connection. No one talks about what they learned or can apply it to their job – they have "been trained" but trained for what? Decades of social science shows us that blaming and shaming people into being inclusive doesn't work. In fact, many diversity and inclusion training programs make people feel more divided and less connected because it provides checklist systems for being "right" or "wrong."

The problem is that we can't motivate people by forcing them to get with the program and punishing them if they don't… It shouldn't be surprising that most diversity programs aren't increasing diversity. Despite a few new bells and whistles, courtesy of big data, companies are basically doubling down on the same approaches they've used since the 1960s – which often make things worse, not better.

Firms have long relied on diversity training to reduce bias on the job, hiring tests and performance ratings to limit it in recruitment and promotions, and grievance systems to give employees a way to challenge managers. Those tools are designed to pre-empt lawsuits by policing managers' thoughts and actions.

Yet laboratory studies show that this kind of force-feeding can activate bias rather than stamp it out. As social scientists have found, people often rebel against rules to assert their autonomy.[44]

If you want to lead an organization where employees feel engaged and included, motivated and driven to use their unique skills and talents to drive performance, then you need to learn how they play. There is no fast-food fix or four-step process that will get you there, and it's not just a check box on an application for funding or government approval. A diverse workforce that connects in play will include *and* perform. After play, they will engage differently, look at their work from a different perspective, and be curious about ways to make change from the inside of your organization that reaches your customers and consumers on the outside. If you want to change direction, you *must* tear down the walls and find the unique and often hidden strengths of your organization.

"A diverse workforce that connects in play will include and perform."

Business is NOT predictable or consistent … PLAY is PRACTICE for risk and reality. Someone said to me today, "I'm always thinking I should be doing something else when I am in play." I responded, "Then you are not IN play … you are doing something that is captivating your time but not your heart." When we play we are enraptured by it; even if it just for a second, we are lost in what we are doing.

If you are a fort builder: share it. If you are a collector: tell people how much you enjoy it. If you are a painter: show the world. Take the time to find your play and let it become powerful beyond measure.

Play will reveal both your company's underlying assumptions – otherwise known as unspoken and unwritten rules – and the talents of the people you work with and for. How you use them to improve performance and profit is a learned skill. In an interview for *WBUR,* Boston's NPR News Station, Sir Ken Robinson said,

> Real creativity comes about through hard work and through application, but not the sort of application that kills the imagination but the kind of work that encourages it. It's a mixture of those two things, of bringing it together — it's a skilled process.[45]

Play is no different. In play, we can open conversations to create divergent thinking and solution-finding. In the process, we reduce the confines of hierarchy and status, which allows us to address the unwritten rules and expectations, which guide all levels of an organization. You will be surprised by the number of staff who will not include their boss in play because they worry about:

- Being seen as unprofessional;
- Judgement on performance; and/or
- Saying or doing something "wrong."

Addressing those concerns alone opens up a space to discuss barriers to employee performance, productivity, and engagement. What is really important is that play takes the lead, so we reduce the fight or flight reactions to discussions about PERFORMANCE, PRODUCTIVITY, AND ENGAGEMENT and get to the very serious underlying issues that build up so many barriers to connection.

Psychological safety is both fragile and vital to organizational success. To create high-impact, sustainable change, we need to address first our natural responses to stress, including the different ways that we cope.

Consider this. If I am an organization funded by a government body and my organization's long-term future is being threatened by budget cuts, then I have a choice: I can worry that my organization will face enormous change and hardship, pass that fear along to my managers and tell them to tighten their belts, to measure every one of their movements, and tell them that <u>their</u> jobs and <u>their</u> security are at risk. They transfer that to their supervisors, who transfer that to their frontline staff. Now everyone is walking around looking for a way to cut corners, to shine brighter, and to be picked for the team. Now everyone is trying to find ways to work harder and longer for less, with less.

And in that process, we compromise trust, honesty, and integrity. Certainly, this changes the way we include or make room for innovation. It changes our perspectives and narrows our choices.

The other choice is this: we can step in with the necessary skills to recognize those "natural" reactions to fear and the unknown. We can choose to build this bridge before it is broken and divided; to know and respect people's anchors, the things that keep them grounded and make them feel complete. We can ensure our first response is based on sharing who we are and the interests that make us whole, rather than the protection of ourselves and our ego. It's vulnerable, and it's risky, but it works.

Great play experiences and sharing can create this. I suggest that play builds psychological safety; that play reveals to us a personal connection that reminds us:

- This person has beliefs, perspectives, and opinions, just like me.

- This person has hopes, anxieties, and vulnerabilities, just like me.
- This person has friends, family, and perhaps children who love them, just like me.
- This person wants to feel respected, appreciated, and competent, just like me.
- This person wishes for peace, joy, and happiness, just like me.[46]

We have lost our sandbox skills: negotiation, conflict management, adaptabilities, innovation. Let's reconnect to those skills, but remember that acknowledging our differences as strengths is a process, not a program.

> *"We have lost our sandbox skills: negotiation, conflict management, adaptabilities, innovation."*

Reconnection

Even the Playing Field - How Play Connects Diversity to Inclusion and Belonging

We met at the corner rink, came from every neighbourhood, represented every age, size, ability, and pocketbook. If we could, we brought extra gear for others so that no one went without, and when they called, "Sticks in the middle!" we all surrendered our sticks, sliding them to the middle of the ice. One of the bigger kids separated the sticks, and you followed your stick to one side of the ice or the other. If you wanted to play, all you had to do was put your stick in the middle.

There are no pictures of this inclusive phenomenon because, at the time, it wasn't considered a way to think about the rights of every player; it was just the way we did it. The story brings tears to my husband's eyes, because, as he recalls, *"It never mattered … when you were the little kid or when you were the big kid, we just knew everyone belonged there."*

Every person has some relationship to inclusion. There are as many definitions of the concept as there are ways to provide it. You may say that you have had no experience at all with inclusion because you define it as "something for people who are marginalized," and that's not your lens. However, if you have ever been invited or not invited to an event, welcomed by strangers into a new space, worked in groups, taken any form of education or training, then you do have a relationship with inclusion. The relationship may be positive and something you remember fondly, or it may be negative and something that makes you hesitant to return. The most important step in creating more inclusive spaces is starting where you are, authentically.

We have started to address diversity by reflecting on who is in the space, who is on the guest list, who is at the top, and who gets to speak. In some areas we have done an excellent job of getting different people into a space to make decisions and create change; in others, we struggle enormously. The road from diversity to inclusion is a long one.

I see diversity and inclusion differently. What I see is that as we create an increased need for standardization, control, and safety, we lose the foundation of what it means to be different, to do it differently, or to see the world from a different perspective. We often see organizations, educators, and teams try to start where they **want to be** instead of **where they are**. More often than not, this creates barriers to building truly inclusive spaces and adopting a more inclusive mindset. In attempting to be more inclusive, we hear about the complexity of required change, ineffective processes, high employee burnout rates, and declining participant satisfaction. High expectations and lack of experience regularly lead us to fast track the process and often results in poor outcomes, unauthentic and unsustainable change.

The idea that inclusion has a defined finish line or list of checkboxes that, once ticked, result in "perfect inclusion" is not representative of reality. Like play, inclusion is a feeling and a way of interacting; it is profoundly personal and as ever-changing as our own life process. What feels inclusive today may not be as inclusive a year from now.

We often shame organizations, services, products, and people for not being more inclusive. However, shaming does not move people toward inclusion but away from it through feeling defeated by what becomes an undefinable process. It's not hard to recognize why diversity and inclusion continue to cause individuals anxiety – we don't want to be seen as unprepared, unqualified, unkind, or uninformed. We race to be where we want to be versus appreciating where we are at.

> *"We often shame organizations, services, products, and people for not being more inclusive. However, shaming does not move people toward inclusion but away from it through feeling defeated by what becomes an undefinable process."*

Inclusion is a journey, not a finish line. I see inclusion as an umbrella, not an arrow.

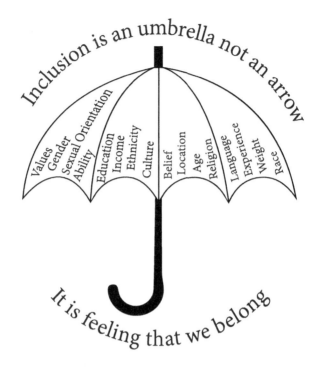

Inclusion is an umbrella not an arrow

Values, Gender, Sexual Orientation, Ability, Education, Income, Ethnicity, Culture, Belief, Location, Age, Religion, Language, Experience, Weight, Race

It is feeling that we belong

So, how is it possible that play can create common ground for such innately personal and complex change? It invites us to go backwards in order to move forward. Play takes us to a space where there are no resources other than our own imagination and creativity. This is why it's so important to play without manufactured toys, arranged play dates, or fancy play equipment. We need more than ever to come to a place where we can imagine without inequity, a place where we

> *"Our level of tolerance for difference, for the unknown, is low. In fact, that bar is on the floor right now, and we are finding all sorts of ways to skirt around it and pretend it isn't there."*

are all the most capable and can use our unique strengths to bring value to the challenge. If you want to build a common ground for real discussion, real change, then I believe there's no better space than play.

Our level of tolerance for difference, for the unknown, is low. In fact, that bar is on the floor right now, and we are finding all sorts of ways to skirt around it and pretend it isn't there. What if we stopped and said …

"Wow! There's a bar on the floor and we need to address it because we keep tripping over it?" instead of continuing to pretend it isn't there until somebody falls, and we blame them? "Didn't you see the bar?" we ask, "You must have known it was there! We told you a million times not to trip over the bar, and you took the 'Bar Recognition Program,' yet the bar is still a problem … why can't you see it?" Despite all this, no one moves it; we leave it there, choosing to ignore it until the next person falls and the cycle restarts.

It's not that people don't know that diversity and inclusion are important; it's that we have screamed it from the rooftops so many times that we no longer know what direction to take. Inclusion has become a finite game of winners and losers, right and wrong. It's over before we even have the chance to ask, "What is **your** experience, **your** understanding, **your** background?" We only know to feel bad if we don't "do it right."

"It's over before we even have the chance to ask, "What is your experience, your understanding, your background?" We only know to feel bad if we don't "do it right.""

We haven't considered working with it instead of around it. Play makes us pick up the bar, name it, work with it, move it, understand it, and make it part of the landscape.

Authentic inclusion is ever-changing. It asks us to consider many perspectives, ways of knowing and doing, failures, and success. One of the major flaws in developing inclusive practice is that one of the key steps is missing: we haven't honestly and authentically processed what scares us, what makes our body and mind go into fight or flight when we see, hear, or feel something different from ourselves. One of the key things play can teach us about inclusion is that bridges are created to invite people from *both* sides. Often, we are uncomfortable with something or someone new because we are stepping onto an unstable bridge, and the person or issue is standing on the other side without the intention of meeting in the middle.

I still hesitate to use a fallen tree to cross running water for fear that it will not hold me or that I am not steady enough, not capable enough to cross. That fear can keep me on one side of the bridge for a long time. Sometimes, I put one foot down and hear something or feel something that makes me pull back to safety. But when I choose "safety," I lose the opportunity to see what's on the other side.

Kids, however, build these kinds of bridges all the time. They build pathways, get wet, rebuild, hold hands, and get across. Consider what would happen if we saw inclusion like a bridge. What if we built bridges that open on both sides? Often, we build how **we** experience, feel, know, and understand on one side. This makes it difficult for us to cross because we haven't discussed that first step: how it can be unsteady, uncomfortable, and even frightening.

Let's return to play ... If we really want to make change, we *must* use our resources to consider all perspectives. We must find rocks to put under our feet and hold hands when we fall. We must look – really look – for solutions that help us *all* cross.

Once the bridge is built, we often cry out in relief, "We did it!!!" and leave it there. We forget to maintain it or fail to predict that the river will rise and fall and take some of our structure away. We forget that a good bridge builds connection to another side, causing us to build one side stronger than the other and, eventually, no one crosses at all.

These bridges are built every day when we meet strangers in the street, face another person in protest, or send texts and social media content. What if we considered the bridge? What are they building their bridge with? Where are they coming from? Where am I coming from? Are we building with the same materials? Facing the same river? How can we come together on the bridge without staying on our own sides in safety?

If you stand on one side of the bridge and say to me, "Shame on you for not knowing, understanding, or connecting to my skills, experience, and background," then the chances that I will come halfway across the bridge to meet you are very small. The opportunity for connection will be lost.

The conversation on inclusion is a bridge that connects us both ways. The knowledge, skills, and ability of the bridge builders change every day – just as intention, words, and actions can be appropriate one day and disgraceful on the next.

Can we come to a place on the bridge where we can say, "I never imagined or intended for my actions, words, or behaviors to hurt you"? And, "I am sorry that they did. Can we learn, connect, and move forward, build a new and better bridge that supports both our needs"? That is a very different discussion than one that starts with, "Shame on you for not building a steady bridge that includes me. You are a bad person."

Unfortunately, the likely response to being shamed for not building an inclusive bridge will be to give up on building any bridge at all. Shaming doesn't build lasting bridges or creative and innovative builders. BUT suppose we learn to play again, to bring all the wrong materials, build terrible first bridges, but try again because we don't feel defeated, shamed, or lost for new ideas. If we do this, we can start to traverse some of our greatest differences again. We can only be as good as learning allows, and learning

"Trying isn't always safe and stable, but staying on one side of the bridge is killing our connection."

requires us to try. Trying isn't always safe and stable, but staying on one side of the bridge is killing our connection.

I believe if we don't step back and address the foundation – the things underneath all the nodding and checkmarks, brochures, and policies that scream, "We are champions of diversity and inclusion!!"; the things that lead us to divide people into stereotypes and categories of who deserves and who doesn't – then we will just continue the cycle: Fear … shame … silence … fear … shame … silence …

"*No matter how many times we try to change the behaviour of people by shaming them for their actions, we haven't a single shred of evidence to say that method works.*"
– *Brené Brown*[47]

So, what if we turn the cycle on its head? Stop shaming and recognize that human beings are driven to belong and to fear things perceived as threatening, unknown, or unheard of. We need to help build skills for navigating and celebrating the new and unknown. What we have is the inability to communicate authentically about our reaction to what's new, diverse, and different from our lens, our reality, our experience. And what's worse, we're slowly structuring this out of kids from a younger and younger age.

I believe if we can rebuild unstructured play as a fundamental aspect of childhood, we can address some of the most vital, underlying challenges of inclusion today:

- Fear of difference;
- Fear of standing out;
- Fear of not standing out;
- Fear of what we don't know;
- Fear of what we can't see;
- Fear of what we don't understand;
- Fear of not knowing;
- Fear of knowing;
- Fear of saying it wrong;
- Fear of saying something about saying it wrong; and
- Fear of feeling.

What if I told you there is no finish line or perfect answer? We are going to get it wrong, and, as with any good strategy, we are going to keep what is working as we continue to evolve alongside the ever-changing and, yes, diverse world we live in.

We need to step back and realize that we need more diverse experiences and exposure to new and diverse people, places, and things. If we don't, we'll continue to create greater and greater divides between what we know and what we are scared of because we don't know. There are people using differences as a weapon to divide others, and the gap between diversity and inclusion gets wider as we introduce more and more fear and intimidation surrounding difference.

"There are people using differences as a weapon to divide others, and the gap between diversity and inclusion gets wider as we introduce more and more fear and intimidation surrounding difference."

It's time to rethink our bridges. How will we ever build resilience and coping if we don't invite difference into our "systems?" We ARE diverse, so let's build skills (not reports) for diversity and for including and for managing our natural reactions to change and fear. If we do this, then we will have something solid to build on.

As a college professor, I often reminded my students that in education (and life), inclusion grows when we start to understand ourselves, what we love, fear, where we have been, and where we want to go. Inclusion means giving ourselves the same grace we extend to others. Inclusion begins with adaptability and flexibility for our differences and unique gifts.

So many people ask me about tools that will help them work in diverse and inclusive settings. I have lots of ideas,1000s really! Almost every one of my adaptations and solutions came from trying and failing many times, from experience, and listening to people first. I had to learn to bend, change, try and fail, and not attach it to my worthiness as a teacher before I could help others find solutions to accessibility, teaching methods, and programming challenges. My willingness to be wrong and learn from my mistakes makes me good at my work. It's playing with the idea that makes it work in the end. If you see every "obstacle" as impossible or a failure of self, you will never find the magic in the opportunity.

What if I told you there is no finish line or perfect answer? We are going to get it wrong, and, as with any good strategy, we are going to keep what is working as we continue to evolve alongside the ever-changing and, yes, diverse world we live in.

We need to step back and realize that we need more diverse experiences and exposure to new and diverse people, places, and things. If we don't, we'll continue to create greater and greater divides between what we know and what we are scared of because we don't know. There are people using differences as a weapon to divide others, and the gap between diversity and inclusion gets wider as we introduce more and more fear and intimidation surrounding difference.

It's time to rethink our bridges. How will we ever build resilience and coping if we don't invite difference into our "systems?" We ARE diverse, so let's build skills (not reports) for diversity and for including and for managing our natural reactions to change and fear. If we do this, then we will have something solid to build on.

As a college professor, I often reminded my students that in education (and life), inclusion grows when we start to understand ourselves, what we love, fear, where we have been, and where we want to go. Inclusion means giving ourselves the same grace we extend to others. Inclusion begins with adaptability and flexibility for our differences and unique gifts.

So many people ask me about tools that will help them work in diverse and inclusive settings. I have lots of ideas,1000s really! Almost every one of my adaptations and solutions came from trying and failing many times, from experience, and listening to people first. I had to learn to bend, change, try and fail, and not attach it to my worthiness as a teacher before I could help others find solutions to accessibility, teaching methods, and programming challenges. My willingness to be wrong and learn from my mistakes makes me good at my work. It's playing with the idea that makes it work in the end. If you see every "obstacle" as impossible or a failure of self, you will never find the magic in the opportunity.

Inclusion starts with "I."

At its highest point, inclusion is expressed as feeling "safe" to speak up without fear of embarrassment or retaliation, *and* when people feel "empowered" to grow and do one's best work. Clearly, these elements are critical for diversity of thinking to emerge.[48]

"Inclusion starts with "I"."

●

What 20 years of Teaching, Leading, and Creating in play has taught me about inclusion:

1. Everyone's performance is affected by what the people around them believe they can do.

2. If you spend your time focused on what people can't do, you'll miss some of their greatest strengths.

3. No one person has all the answers; life is a collaborative effort.

4. Until we address our conscious and unconscious fears around difference, we won't be able sustain inclusive practice. What we fear is often greater than our motivation to change the social script.

5. Everyone has the ability when they feel valued and valuable.

6. Inclusion is a feeling, like belonging; it only grows when we let ourselves be seen.

Generation Play – Permission to Play Again

To watch her play is mesmerizing. The steady flow of her hands in the dirt, how she touches everything with care and a reverence for its worth holds my gaze. Everything surrounding her is growing and changing. She sits in what looks like an uncomfortable position until you realize it's the way she can access the greatest number of items at one time and still stay in balance. Captured by the smell of the grass and the dirt under her nails, she spends timeless hours dedicated to what would seem to some an endless task. It is her play; she is lost in it and is occasionally heard singing or humming while she works. This is my mother's garden. It is where she disappears beyond time, or pain, or the weight she carries for herself and others. The garden renews and reconnects her energy and strength to bounce back and keep going. She is play-grounded in her garden. She is Sage: wise through reflection and experience.

"She is Sage: wise through reflection and experience."

We are living longer, and a longer life brings with it opportunities – not only for older people and their families but for societies as a whole. Additional years provide the chance to pursue new activities such as further education, a new career, or a long-neglected passion. But in order to fulfill that potential for a full life, we need to give older adults permission to play again. This includes providing playful opportunities as well as considering how we see them and how they see themselves.

What if we changed the script for older adults to say, "*This* is the time to pursue your play. Do things that make you feel confident and competent, build again, laugh, sing, learn something new, just … play!" But we don't. Unfortunately, we bubble wrap them and protect them, and then we ask why we have the highest rates of loneliness and depression among older adults. What if we said this is your time to explore and systemically opened doors and attitudes towards aging as an opportunity? For instance, how many times do we say to our parents, "I wouldn't do that, it's too risky," or, "You should slow down," or, "Do what's safe"? So many adults older than me tell me that unstructured, un-watched, unobstructed play was how they played when they were children, but not very many say they still play like that now. Why not? Because it's been organized right out of them. A lifetime of doing what was expected, following the rules and a schedule, has drained their drive to play. For some, it's reignited in being grandparents – even the most stringent CEO can be found on the floor pretending, singing, and inventing with their grandchild(ren). You see, there is this wonderful thing that happens with children: they give us back our permission to play. We are transformed by watching the ease with which they create, the wonder in simple discoveries, and the carelessness with which they navigate their worlds. Play opens the door for translation, connection, and curiosity when given an invitation.

When we watch generations of people play through unstructured, unfacilitated activates, we can see this translation take place. When grandparents build forts from couch cushions and turn wooden sticks into swords, they communicate to their grandchildren, "This is how we used to play." In that moment, there is connection. Play teaches the value of experience to younger generations and reminds older generations of the value of curiosity and discovery.

Let's apply those same principles of risky play to our lives as we age. We need to support – not suspend – exploration as we age, and we need to start with how we address aging as a society so that we can start speaking to ourselves with greater respect and grace.

●

Years ago, I assisted a client with her supervised exercise program after a fall. One day, while we were working on lifting, I asked her to pick up one of the 2 lb weights from the shelf.

She looked at me with surprise and said, "I can't lift that. I'm 80 you know!" I laughed a little and asked her who bought the groceries in her house.

"I do!" she proudly exclaimed.

So, I asked her what she bought this week. She gave me the whole list: butter, eggs, a turkey, her husband's favourite canned ham, and more. Doing a rough calculation in my head, I estimated at least 6 lbs of groceries and asked her, "What makes you think you can't lift that weight?"

"Weights are for young people," she replied, "It's what teenagers do, not grandmas."

I told her, "You are stronger than you believe!" and distributed 4 lbs between two grocery bags for her to carry on our walk. Our perspective of aging is often challenged by how we see ourselves.

Ask yourself, *What are some of the limiting thoughts and ideas I have about aging? Is one or many of them about risk? Resilience? Strength? Play?* Let's expect more of ourselves and others.

The Rubber Shark Principle

> *If you put a soccer ball down in the middle of a circle of adults and ask, "What do we do with this?" someone or, depending on the group, many people will kick the ball. Most people will start to pass it around the circle with their feet. They will continue to pass among the group, trying their best to complete the expected action: kick the ball to someone else. People who feel confident will be smiling and even laughing as they kick the ball with ease to others and almost will the ball to come back – this is their play. However, there will be others who will try their best but are not invested in the activity; people who will eventually become bored by the process – this isn't their play.*

There will almost always be people in the group who are not excited by the prospect of kicking the ball. In fact, their entire body language says, "Please don't pass it to me!" But, because we have been taught to give everyone a turn, the ball will eventually make it to them. Their body and mind work against them here for many reasons: they may have no experience with kicking (perhaps because they've had a bad experience with kicking), or they may fear not "looking" like a kicker, missing the ball completely, or sending it to someone inadvertently. I can add to this stress by making everyone say who they are going to pass to, or I can reduce the stress by keeping it random.

Notice I have said nothing yet about soccer, but if I ask, "Who is a soccer player?" I can add on layers of social expectation. Who does or does not consider themselves official soccer players? Who played as a kid? Who still plays now? I can create a system of classes with a single question.

However, if I take a circle of adults and throw a rubber shark in the middle and ask, "What do we do with this?" nine times out of ten, someone will pick it up and throw it to someone else. The same cycle ensues, only this time almost all are smiling, and there is no tension, no turning away, no heads down. Do you know why? There are no social, cognitive, or physical expectations attached to the rubber shark. No one played on the National Shark Throwing Team, no one knows the best way, or the right way, or has more experience than others throwing the rubber shark. This means no one is watching with judgement or rating your skill. Instead, our minds are open to the possibility of not only dropping it but laughing about how we do it.

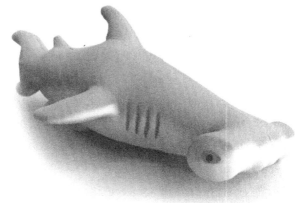

You see, the Rubber Shark Principle is this: when we create space for every person's way of doing and knowing, we are open to so many more opportunities and possibilities. Sometimes even the simplest things have complex, preconceived agendas, so let's put out the rubber shark more often so that everyone can contribute and choose to play.

The 6S (Success) Of Play

I carry a bag of "tools" in an old rolling suitcase to most of my work. I do this in community, in teaching, and in presenting. It is my version of a good Swiss Army Knife. You know … the kind that can open a can, sew a button, fix your glasses, and open every tightly wrapped gift. My grandfather always had one in his pocket. And for good reason: it always came in handy!

I grew up in a world of limitless exploration. Both my father and my grandfather were fixers and artists in their own right. My father is an artist and a dreamer, and his love for making something out of nothing is a skill I'm ever grateful for. Our basement was perfectly unfinished as it was both a studio and a playroom. I remember turning sawdust into paint texture with my dad and using the cut off ends of frames for my own building creations. My dad didn't teach me how to paint; he just gave me the materials to find my own talent. I learned early on that everything had a purpose, even before recycling was cool!

This skill followed me into the world of work as I always had a knack for mending and connecting: sometimes people, sometimes things. I rarely go anywhere without access to a pool noodle and a box of crayons.

PLAY6S was built on the basics of Adapted Physical Education and Therapeutic Play, experience, and lots of help from the 1000s of children, families, and students I have had the honour to work with over the years. I don't work in diagnosis and labels, so I won't claim people with autism experience this or that or people living with mental illness prefer one space to another. Instead, I teach people to ask, observe, and connect the 6Ss to every person and to recognize that no group of people – no matter how similar their experience – prefer or are sensitive to the 6Ss equally. People are always curious about how I come up with solutions and adaptations for physical activity skills and experiences that enable every person to participate. PLAY6S was built on trying to find a solution that could easily be remembered and implemented.

There are six 6S: Surface, Size, Space, Sound, Support, and Speed. The 6S principles encompass not only physical adaptions but the whole person, cognitive, social, emotional and sensory adaptations are part of 6S full adaptation.

1. Surface. What is beneath you, what are you grounded to? Do you love sand or water? Grass or hardwood? Which one is easier to move on or in? Which one provides resistance or challenge? Consider things we touch every day – from taps on a keyboard to blankets at night. What is it that draws you to one or the other? We can use this type of discovery play to build everything from fundamental movement skills to customer service. Consider all the different surfaces you come into contact with every day and which one you prefer.

2. Size. This includes considering everything from the size of the type on a set of instructions to the size of the ball you are throwing. Consider something personal like a wallet or a cell phone. What size do you prefer? How long does it take you to get used to a new one if it's a different size?

Are there some you've given up because you couldn't get used to them? Size and weight go together. Consider shoes or coats: think about their weight and function and how wearing the wrong weight or size can change how you process the day. Consider rubber boots versus flip flops, heavy winter jackets versus spring coats.

3. Space. Consider for a minute your bubble: the distance you keep between yourself and a stranger. Have you ever had someone too close? Too far away? It can change our connection, communication, and learning. What is your favourite type of space? Is it crowded, busy, solitary, or quiet? Success comes from recognizing the different ways we feel comfortable. When are you comfortable enough to be yourself and play?

4. Sound. This one is easy,… or is it? Consider what you hear or don't hear every day. Being unable to decipher what someone is saying by the volume of their voice is just one example of how sound can change our experience. Have you ever left a room full of people because it makes you feel exhausted? Processing sound, especially from multiple sources, can be very tiring and overwhelming. For people who live with sensitivities to sound, it can be unbearable. PLAY 6S reminds us to take a moment to consider how we process sound physically, cognitively, and emotionally so that we can address the needs and preferences of the people we work and play with.

5. Support. Physical support can look like a hand to hold, feel like a safety net, and sound like "1, 2, 3 … go!" When it

comes to support, we want to know what people need that motivates them to move forward – both independently and interdependently. Cognitive support could be providing clear instructions, visual schedules, or auditory prompts/cues, while social support is about building self-regulation and negotiation skills. Emotional support comes in many forms, including touch, facial expression, encouragement, and trust.

6. Speed. What is your speed? When someone explains something to you, do you want them to rush through the instructions so you can try it yourself, or do you want all the details before you start? If you consider the increasing pace of change and technology, are you thrilled by the opportunities or, do you cautiously inquire at every level? What is your reaction time – not just physically (for example, how you would react if I threw a ball to you unexpectedly) but mentally (for example, how you process new information). When your body and mind process something new, how fast do you recover? If you are concentrating and suddenly called to do something new and unexpected, how long does it take you to recalibrate? When we played games like Simon Says and What Time Is It Mr. Wolf as children, we practiced changing our actions and intentions with a moment's notice. I suggest that we have lost our motivation to practice these skills in relation to our expectations for people to consistently adapt "on the fly."

The 6Ss ask us to be curious about more than what we can see! Asking questions about each of the 6Ss reminds us that we all have preferences and different methods for learning, moving, and thinking. The 6Ss are physical (movement, coordination, reaction time), cognitive (how we process information, remember, pay attention), social (connecting and responding), and emotional (how we feel). When we consider how to make a workspace, program, or classroom more inclusive and adaptable using the 6Ss, we look first at the ways in which people experience the space or activity. Almost everything can be modified to create a more accessible activity or space by considering the 6S Principles.

So, how do we navigate all of this in play? Be prepared to be deeply curious again and consider solutions for you and others that are new and inventive. PLAY6S means considering multiple lenses through which to see solutions and innovations that lead to both progress AND transition. Your greatest challenge will be to start with you! When you examine your personal PLAY6S, you will open doors to seeing how it manifests in others. We don't teach people to play; we reveal their play by first being open to our potential and then helping others be open to theirs.

"Be prepared to be deeply curious again and consider solutions for you and others that are new and inventive."

Not a Conclusion … It's Just The Beginning

I want to be able to walk into a room full of people one day and ask, "When was the last time you remember playing"? And without filters or fear people answer back with abundant answers, sharing where and when they were "in play". People answering without considering what they "should say" or they are supposed to say or expected to say. I want people to discover that they all have an answer. We can move from *online* to *in line* with empathy and connection by starting to reconnect people of all ages to the playful parts of themselves and their worlds.

What if we don't change, don't return to play? We may choose not to draw, or move, or dance, or sing, or build, or discover without instructions, security, and stability in a world that requires us to imagine, risk, and change. We might miss the chance to explore something that makes our spirit soar,or an opportunity to connect with people we do not know. We might not paint the frames, or find our motivation to get to tomorrow, or try one more time.

Stop to consider your play today. Do it without judgement, without hesitation, knowing that it is the key to your greatest potential. Now bring it to your day for one minute, do it once a day, look for it when you walk down the street or buy groceries, and smile when you see it in others. Eventually, you will seek longer moments of it, and you will

"Play is contagious. Let's share it!"

give yourself and others permission to play again. Play is contagious. Let's share it!

Notes

1   Picture Perfect Playgrounds, Inc. (2020). *Swinging.* https://www.pgpedia.com/s/swinging

2   Picture Perfect Playgrounds, "Swinging."

3   Brown, S. (2009). *Play: How it shapes the brain, opens the imagination and invigorates the soul.* Penguin Publishing Group.

4   Carroll, K. (2012, July 27). *Play is necessary: Kevin Carroll at TEDxHarlem* [Video]. TED Conferences. https://www.youtube.com/watch?v=1pz72Wygg8c

5   Seth Godin, personal communication, September 15, 2020.

6   Daniel Pink, electronic communication, September 6, 2020.

7   Sandseter, E. B. H., & Kennair, L. E. O. (2011). Children's risky play from an evolutionary perspective: The anti-phobic effects of thrilling experiences. *Evolutionary Psychology,* 9(2), 257-284. https://doi.org/10.1177/147470491100900212

8   Brown, S., & Vaughan, C. (2009). Play: *How it shapes the brain, opens the imagination, and invigorates the soul.* Penguin Group.

9   Delizonna, L. (2017, August 24). High-performing teams need psychological safety. Here's how to create it. *Harvard Business Review.* Retrieved from https://hbr.org/2017/08/high-performing-teams-need-psychological-safety-heres-how-to-create-it

10   Hanscom, A. J. (2016). Balanced and barefoot: How unrestricted outdoor play makes for strong, confident, and capable children. New Harbinger Publications, Inc.

11   Tremblay, M. S., Gray, C., Babcock, S., Barnes, J., Bradstreet, C. C., Carr, D., Chabot, G., Choquette, L., Chorney, D., Collyer, C., Herrington, S., Janson, K., Janssen, I., Larouche,

R., Pickett, W., Power, M., Sandseter, E. B. H., Simon, B., & Brussoni, M. (2015). Position statement on active outdoor play. *International Journal of Environmental Research and Public Heath,* 12, 6475-6505. doi:10.3390/ijerph120606475

12   World Health Organization. (2018, February 23). *Physical activity.* https://www.who.int/news-room/fact-sheets/detail/physical-activity

13   World Health Organization. (2019, April, 24). *To grow up healthy, children need to sit less and play more* [News release]. https://www.who.int/news-room/detail/24-04-2019-to-grow-up-healthy-children-need-to-sit-less-and-play-more

14   Gray, P. (2013). Free to learn: *Why unleashing the instinct to play will make our children happier, more self-reliant, and better students for life.* Basic Books.

15   Discovering the importance of play through personal histories and brain images: An interview with Stuart L. Brown. (2009). *American Journal of Play,* 1(4), 399-412. Retrieved from https://eric.ed.gov/?id=EJ1069017

16   Elkind, D. (2007). *The power of play: What comes naturally.* Da Capo Press.

17   Michael Yogman, Andrew Garner, Jeffrey Hutchinson, Kathy Hirsh-Pasek, Roberta Michnick Golinkoff, COMMITTEE ON PSYCHOSOCIAL ASPECTS OF CHILD AND FAMILY HEALTH, COUNCIL ON COMMUNICATIONS AND MEDIA. The power of play: a pediatric role in enhancing development in young children. Pediatrics Sep 2018, 142 (3) e20182058; DOI: 10.1542/peds.2018-2058

18   GOV.UK. (2018, October 16). *Prime Minister Theresa May launches government's first loneliness strategy* [Press release].   https://www.gov.uk/government/news/pm-launches-governments-first-loneliness-strategy

19   Schäfer, K., Saarikallio, S., & Eerola, T. (2020). Music may reduce loneliness and act as social surrogate for a friend: Evidence

from an experimental listening study. *Music & Science*, 3, 1-16. https://doi.org/10.1177/2059204320935709

20 Online Etymology Dictionary. (n.d.). *Humility.* Retrieved June, 05, 2020 from https://www.etymonline.com/word/humility#etymonline_v_16050

21 Grenberg, J. (2005). *Kant and the ethics of humility: A story of dependence, corruption, and virtue.* Cambridge University Press.

22 Brown, S. (2009). *Play: How it shapes the brain, opens the imagination and invigorates the soul.* Penguin Publishing Group.

23 Spiegel, A. (2008, February 21). *Old-fashioned play builds serious skills.* National Public Radio. https://www.npr.org/templates/story/story.php?storyId=19212514

24 World Health Organization. (2018, March 30). *Mental health: Strengthening our response.* https://www.who.int/news-room/fact-sheets/detail/mental-health-strengthening-our-response

25 Entin, E. (2011, October 12). All work and no play: Why your kids are more anxious, depressed. *The Atlantic.* https://www.theatlantic.com/health/archive/2011/10/all-work-and-no-play-why-your-kids-are-more-anxious-depressed/246422/

26 Whitebread, D. (2017, November 1). Free play and children's mental health. *The Lancet: Child & Adolescent Health,* 1(3), 167-169. https://doi.org/10.1016/S2352-4642(17)30092-5

27 Silvestro, S. (2012, May 2). Patch Adams on the power of play and living a life of joy [Audio podcast]. Retrieved from https://www.drstevesilvestro.com/patch-adams#:~:text=%E2%80%9CEven%20in%20the%20worst%20of,enjoy%20play.%E2%80%9D%20%E2%80%93%20Patch%20Adams

28 Seth Godin, personal communication, September 15, 2020.

29 AMPED2PLAY. (2019) Ramshackle play: *In diversity & inclusion, education & community.* https://amped2play.com/

service/ramshackle-play/

30   Sandseter, E. B. H. (2007). Categorizing risky play – How can we identify risk-taking in children's play? *European Early Childhood Education Research Journal,* 15(2), 237-252. http://www.tandfonline.com/doi/abs/10.1080/13502930701321733#.VTDjW2ccSUk

31   Sandseter & Kennair, "Children's risky play from an evolutionary perspective."

32   Merriam-Webster. (n.d.). *Foreplay.* Retrieved September, 20, 2020 from https://www.merriam-webster.com/dictionary/foreplay

33   Sinek, S. (2019). *The infinite game.* SinekPartners, LLC.

34   Coyle, D. (2018). *The culture code:* The secrets of highly successful groups. Bantam Books.

35   Thiessen, M., Gluth, S., & Corso, R. (2013). Unstructured play and creative development in the classroom. *International Journal for Cross-Disciplinary Subjects in Education,* 4(4), 1341-1348. Retrieved from https://infonomics-society.org/wp-content/uploads/ijcdse/published-papers/voulme-4-2013/Unstructured-Play-and-Creative-Development-in-the-Classroom.pdf

36   Seth Godin, personal communication, September 15, 2020.

37   Gray, P. (2008, November 19). The value of play I: The definition of play gives insights: Freedom to quit is an essential aspect of play's definition. *Psychology Today.* https://www.psychologytoday.com/ca/blog/freedom-learn/200811/the-value-play-i-the-definition-play-gives-insights

38   Seth Godin, personal communication, September 15, 2020.

39   Robinson, K., & Aronica, L. (2009). *The element: How finding your passion changes everything.* Penguin Books.

40   Save Our Future (n.d.). Retrieved September, 12, 2020 from https://saveourfuture.world/

41   Whitehead, M. (2016). The value of physical literacy.

Retrieved September 6, 2016 from https://www.physical-literacy. org.uk/value-physical-literacy/

42   Rozovsky, J. (2015, November 17). The five keys to a successful Google team. re: *Work*. https://rework.withgoogle. com/blog/five-keys-to-a-successful-google-team/

43   Wigert, B., & Robison, J. (2018, December 19). Fostering creativity at work: Do your managers push or crush innovation? Gallup. https://www.gallup.com/workplace/245498/ fostering-creativity-work-managers-push-crush-innovation. aspx#:~:text=Only%2029%25%20of%20workers%20 strongly,to%20do%20things%20at%20work.&text=It's%20 flattering%20to%20be%20applauded,can%20lead%20to%20- big%20things.

44   Dobbin, F., & Kalev, A. (2016, July 5). How to make your organisation more diverse. *The Financial Review*. https://www. afr.com/work-and-careers/management/how-to-make-your- organisation-more-diverse-20160621-gpofio

45   Clayson, J. (2013, June 19). Sir Ken Robinson on discovering your passions. WBUR: On Point. https://www.wbur. org/onpoint/2013/06/19/sir-ken-robinson

46   Delizonna, "High-performing teams need psychological safety."

47   Brown, B. (2013). *The power of vulnerability: Teaching on authenticity, connection and courage.* (B. Brown, Narr.) [Audiobook]. Sounds True.

48   Bourke, J., & Dillon, B. (2018, January 22). The diversity and inclusion revolution: Eight powerful truths. *Deloitte Review,* https://www2.deloitte.com/us/en/insights/deloitte-review/ issue-22/diversity-and-inclusion-at-work-eight-powerful-truths. html